The Uncanny Grasp of The Obvious

To have an uncanny grasp of the obvious is the ability to see things that people often overlook or take for granted. It allows us to dig deeper into the reality of our lives and to discover that which often seems so commonplace, can be quite complex. In this collection of entertaining and insightful essays, poems, and stories, the authors delve into the very imaginative as well as the most mundane aspects of our world. Gleaned from their professional experiences as well as casual encounters with others, they explore everything from the roundness of tires, inventory taking robots, ghost stories, belief in ESP, to music, getting older, and social justice. While the narrative presentation may at times be light-hearted or satirical, and at other times more serious in nature, these essays provide a metaphor for more profound aspects of our living–and nothing is as obvious as it seems.

"When do people stop being curious? In this collection of essays, Scott and Dean allow their minds to wander, following interesting and thought-provoking tangents along a variety of topics, questioning and discovering the curiosities that cross their minds... By '...always being curious, being creative, and always finding something interesting in our lives and the lives of others... We realize that life is a gift that provides interesting experiences.' May their writing inspire your own curiosity."

> – Heather McEndree, Executive Director at
> Cumberland Valley School of Music

"This book is an enjoyable and thoughtful read by observant storytellers. *The Uncanny Grasp of the Obvious* leads us to insightful forays into our own thoughts, and takes us along new pathways with glimpses of gleaming colors available to the mindful. The authors ask 'creative questions,' encouraging us to 'think like an artist;' exploring 'What might be possible?' And, 'What are the next steps in our personal journey?'"

> – Andrea Ros, Artist - Apocalypse Carousel Project

"As I live the life of a retired fine arts and art history professor, making an effort to further engage with community and make every day meaningful, *The Uncanny Grasp of the Obvious* has opened new windows for me as I continue, after forty years of teaching, to note that our lives will thrive as long as we use creativity in our shared humanity! This book will be a fascinating resource for me. I highly recommend this read!"

    – Greg Winterhalter, Visual Artist and Professor Emeritus, Southern Vermont College

"In one of the essays the authors' present an understanding of how music can transport you anywhere, especially when you are 'in the groove.' Maybe if more of us were in the groove, we would understand each other and empathize more... then the world would be a better place."

    – Sandra Zupanski, J.D.

The Uncanny Grasp of the Obvious

Scott F. Madey and Dean D. VonDras

The Uncanny Grasp of the Obvious

† Imprimatur Bonheur & Rire LLC - United States

ISBN EBook: 979-8-9900884-3-6
ISBN Paperback: 979-8-9900884-4-3
Library of Congress Control Number: 2025917153

First Edition

Cover art by D. D. VonDras, "At the Crossing," 2025, mixed media.

The information presented herein represent the opinions, creative work, and imaginative stories of the Authors as of the publication date. Thus, this book is presented for entertainment and information purposes only, and not intended as a substitute for expert advice or assistance from a licensed professional. While every attempt has been made to verify the accuracy of the information presented, the Publisher and Authors assume no responsibility for any inaccuracies, errors,

Table of Contents

Preface

As we go through life, we observe the world around us. At times these observations can inspire us to react in rather profound ways. They can elicit deep reflections on life's great meaning and may change the direction our lives take or the paths we follow. At other times these observations may go rather unexamined and we may determine that they require no further scrutiny. In this book, we want to highlight that maybe it is those observations, seemingly of little importance or quite obvious, that may hold the greatest insight into who we are as a person and a society. Before we begin our exploration of the obvious, we would like to tell the reader a little bit about ourselves and how we came to know each other and then explain the intention of our book.

How We Came to Know Each Other

We have been friends and collaborators for almost 30 years. From 1995 to 1998, as post-docs, we worked together studying the process of getting older. During that time, we published several articles mostly about how older adults attain health goals. After our post-doc stint, we both went our separate ways and were not in touch again until around 2017, when Dean contacted me and asked if I would contribute a chapter to a book he was editing on spirituality and health: *Better Health Through Spiritual Practices: A Guide to Religious Behaviors and Perspectives That Benefit Mind and Body* (2017). I had retired at that time and was certainly experiencing the transition from a regular work schedule to something driven by where I placed my interest and effort. I agreed. After that, we re-established regular contact and started tossing around ideas on aging, and what it means to become "older." We began hammering out the ideas of what a book that incorporated our love of music would say about getting older and staying healthy. This work evolved over the years and culminated in the book *Music, Wellness, and Aging: Defining, Directing, and Celebrating Life* (2021). We somewhat jokingly remark to each other that the book took 3 years to write but a lifetime of experience to be able to write it. Our next book, *Celebrating the Arts of Living: Pathways to Joy and Fulfillment in Later Life* (2024) could possibly be the "sequel" to the previous book in that we expand our considerations of what contributes to life satisfaction and ultimately a celebration of life through artistic expression. We believe that it is through the stories and lives of people that we see the wonder of human resilience and the process of becoming who we are ultimately meant to be. Our latest work, which we hope you are about to read, is titled *The Uncanny Grasp of the Obvious*.

The phrase that someone has an uncanny grasp of the obvious is quite curious. Many years ago, one of us was taking a graduate seminar and was commenting on the assigned reading when the professor, with a wry smile quipped, "I'm amazed that you have such an uncanny grasp of the obvious!" Understanding this professor's sense of humor and not to be taken aback, the immediate response was "Thank you, I am glad you appreciate that not everyone has this gift!" When we were discussing how we would write this book, the professor's remark made so many years ago came to mind. We concluded that to understand the obvious is a skill that is often under-appreciated. Indeed, having an uncanny grasp of the obvious is a testament to our powers of observation and the ability to see those things that people often overlook or take for granted. It allows us to dig deeper into our lives and to discover that what seems so commonplace, or "obvious" can be quite complex.

We want to emphasize that this work is not intended as an overly wrought academic text or research book. Written for the lay reader as well as aspiring student, the essays we present are often colloquial in nature, sharing our observations and insights, and composed in a style so as to embrace the enjoyment and fun of considering new ideas and continuing to learn at any age. Thus, the narrative presentation may at times be light-hearted or satirical, and at other times more serious in nature. The topics and insights discussed have their genesis in our teaching psychology, involvement as musicians, as well as what we saw on the internet, learned about in casual meetings and informal social gatherings, or gleaned from encounters in the grocery store. Here, we delve into and share the very imaginative as well as most mundane aspects of our world, hoping the reader will find our discussion insightful and come away with an understanding of something special.

Indeed, often in the process of writing, something unique emerges that is very different from what one had originally planned. What we thought would be essays written from a satirical, humorous, or quirky point of view, upon reading became a metaphor for more profound aspects of living. We guess in a way, a reflection on the obvious brought out the complexities of life—nothing is as obvious as it seems. Perhaps in reading these essays, you, the reader, may gain an insight into something that did not occur to you, and elicit a new perspective, a new way of seeing your world. Thus, we encourage you to find something of your own experiences in these stories that will inspire you to reflect on the happy, sad, funny, and hopeful times in your own lives. Because, to have an uncanny grasp of the obvious is a gift that allows us to see the beauty of the world, to appreciate people we love and who love us, and to find wonderment in the commonness of our shared experiences. We hope that you enjoy these essays on the obvious.

Acknowledgements

It is obviously important to acknowledge that this work reflects the authors' personal experiences and subjective recollections. Thus, at times the remembrance of conversations have been recreated and/or supplemented for narrative purposes, and names and identifying details may have been omitted or changed to protect the privacy of individuals. Further, and for very obvious reasons, we note that the views and opinions offered in this book are solely those of the authors and are not intended to harm or defame any person, living or dead. We also acknowledge that some or all of the parts of the imaginative stories found in, "A Funny Thing Happened on the Way to a Concert in the Park," "A Terrifying Ghost Story," "Cast as a Non-Speaking Character: A Short Story," and "Epilogue: A Call from the Local Community Theater," as well as the prose pieces, "I Saw Truth," "Not Uncommon Experience," and "The Circus," are works of fiction. Unless otherwise indicated, all the names, characters, businesses, places, events and incidents in these stories and prose pieces are either the product of the author's imagination or used in a fictitious manner. Any resemblance to actual persons, living or dead, or actual events is purely coincidental.

We further acknowledge and wish to thank reviewers for their helpful comments and suggestions.

We also wish to acknowledge and thank our parents and teachers, whose caring guidance continues to inspire us and makes this work possible. We similarly express thanks to brothers and sisters, nieces and nephews, and our entire family, whose love and support is deeply appreciated.

Lastly, very special thanks go to Paula Madey, and Mary Elizabeth and Jack VonDras, for their sustaining love and encouragement throughout this project, and in our journey in life together.

Scott F. Madey and Dean D. VonDras

Chapter 1 – The Uncanny Grasp of the Obvious

It is important to give the reader a clear idea of what it means to have an uncanny grasp of the obvious. As we see in the essay that opens this chapter by Scott that to have an uncanny grasp of the obvious is a gift, an insight into our everyday world that may often go unobserved by others and its implications for how we evaluate the profoundness or silliness of the observations we make. Next, Scott, in the essay "Analog People..." writes about his encounter with an inventory taking robot in a grocery store that leads to a reflection on AI technology and our survival as a species. Scott's essay on how to play well with other musicians and what it means to establish a groove is then presented. In the story, "A Funny Thing Happened..." Dean discusses a fictional experience when he and his family attend a concert in the park and concludes that music is important for community cohesiveness. Finally, the chapter closes with a poem "The Circus" by Scott that reflects in a somewhat detached way how we observe others and ends with a realization of the meaning of one's life.

* * *

The Uncanny Grasp of the Obvious

It takes a special type of insight to understand the obvious. But wait, the reader might ask that isn't what is obvious, something that requires no insight? It is just obvious. We like to think that we can recognize the obvious. But it is not as easy as it seems. The Psychologist, Richard Farson points out that the obvious often is quite invisible to us. This idea implies that somehow the obvious must go through a process to reveal itself. The counterintuitive quality of the obvious is further exemplified by Arthur Conan Doyle's fictional character Sherlock Holmes who observed that if we recognize something as obvious, we are probably being deceived. We also may consider examples where someone is totally unaware of the obvious. We see this commonly played out in love stories, where a person is in a relationship with another but fails to recognize that the other person is in love with them. Or we can describe a situation, possibly the threat of an upcoming war, or financial disaster that when it happens totally takes us by surprise. Common parlance in these examples, are statements such as "a failure to see what is in front of one's face," or "How did I not see this coming?" But for some reason, after the event occurs, it becomes obvious–how could one not have seen it as inevitable?

But then another component of this discussion of the obvious involves what it means when one finally sees something with certainty, clarity, and inevitability? Interestingly, someone with this insight can look both smart and stupid. Insight into the obvious when it comes to predicting wars, financial collapse, or love affairs can raise the person to a high status, as an expert, a vanguard, someone ahead of their time, particularly to those "who did not see it coming." However, if one quips that "tires are round." This claim is not only obvious but inherently not profound and will result in the person being viewed by others as rather silly (the stupid side of the argument). I will point out that such a statement is not as silly–or as obvious–as it seems. In fact, declarations of the inevitability of war or the roundness of tires have the same underlying themes.

An interesting phenomenon in psychology is the hindsight bias. The hindsight bias states that after an event has occurred, we now have a strong belief that we could have predicted the outcome before it had happened. At least three things occur in hindsight. One is that we believe we can now connect all the dots that led up to the outcome. Another thing that allows us to connect the dots is that a causal chain of events is strengthened and is strongly linked to the outcome after the fact. Finally, in hindsight we filter out the noise of other information, ideas, or data that existed before the outcome that are now deemed to be unrelated to the outcome. We can think of events such as 9/11, the stock market crash of 1929, or the bombing of Pearl Harbor in World War II as being more obvious after they happened than before. Hindsight is not only a bias in our ability to have foreseen the future, but it also affects how we see others. With the benefit of hindsight, we cannot understand why others could not see the same outcome. In effect, these folks over-predict how well they "saw it coming." Thus, the obvious emerges in hindsight when the causal connections of events are made stronger after the event has occurred.

A second theme is that what is obvious to someone may not be obvious to someone else. Thus, the stuff of love stories or the prediction of major events. The person initially unaware of the obviousness of the situation and becomes aware of it may be viewed by the other as stating something that is or should be abundantly clear to everyone. This interaction folds into the previous discussion that the "informed" person possibly has engaged in a hindsight bias. But also brings into discussion that once something becomes obvious and common knowledge, that a statement of it, although personally insightful, is not very exciting or earth-shattering news–like the tires are round example. But if we think about our silly example that tires are round, it is not so silly when we study the history of transportation and technological advancements that led to the invention of the tire–which is indeed, a deceptively obvious fact!

The title of this essay is the Uncanny Grasp of the Obvious. The word uncanny can describe something weird, strange, mysterious, or difficult to explain. The use of the word uncanny can also refer to an extraordinary skill or ability. Both apply. Indeed, the grasp of the obvious is a strange and wonderful ability to have whether predicting major events or commenting on the roundness of tires.

* * *

Analog People in a Digital World: Or, Why I No Longer Fear AI

I was in the local grocery store when I first saw "Bob." Bob was this robot-looking thing about 7 feet tall, bluish-gray color with blinking lights for eyes. It casually glided up and down the aisles of the store. Bob also seemed quite harmless and quite friendly-looking. Intrigued, I walked up to Bob and said what I thought was a humorous remark: "Hey Bob, there's a cleanup needed in aisle three." Bob ignored me and moved on. I thought that maybe he had more important business to attend to. I never did find out what Bob's job was except to glide up and down the aisles.

Another store too had a robot with a less gender specific name, "Tally." Having learned my lesson on robot protocol from Bob, I first looked at the printing on Tally's body. It said "Hi, I'm Tally. I conduct in-store inventory." I saw then that Tally would stop at the end of an aisle or by a bin and a little beep and a blink of lights would happen, indicating that the important work of counting the merchandise was in good hands. Therefore, I did not attempt to interrupt Tally.

After my encounters with Bob and Tally, I began to think more about discussions on how AI is a danger and may possibly take over society. Also, there is a fear that AI may become so advanced that we will not be able to distinguish a real person from something generated by AI. One can now think about what we call deep fakes where AI technology is used to impersonate a person, usually someone famous. Other examples, and the bane of teachers and educators is ChatGPT, and other AI programming. With a bit of input, one can generate a paper, musical composition, artistic painting, etc. You could ask AI to play, paint, compose "in the style of ..."

and AI will produce something. One could even program it to play guitar in my style–but who would want to! At least for now, many of these can be identified as obvious products of AI. And AI detection programs exist. But there may come a time when we will not be able to spot the difference. This is where a singularity occurs. And more ominously, this is where the machine acquires full sentience. The implication of the singularity for us is that the rise of AI dominance will force humankind to either evolve or give our freedom over to computers and machines (think about the movies *Terminator*, *The Matrix*, *I Robot*, or *BladeRunner*). We may have to one day give our allegiance to "Bob" (or a Bob-like machine), but I certainly cannot predict when that will occur. Also, I do not fear the singularity happening anytime soon (I may be wrong, of course). My reasoning is a little more personal and it comes down to loopers and drummers.

Over my years of guitar playing, I used very few effects. At the most I used maybe fuzz, overdrive, delay, and wah-wah pedals. Now I go from guitar straight to the amp. Sometimes I would use a delay, but I am still very minimalistic. Although I tried a looper, I found that I could not use it well enough in a performance situation, but I do find a looper quite useful to first lay down a chord pattern when I want to work on a lead part. In performance, however, I would lay down the chords, but when I began to play the second guitar part, or the lead, I would forget to press the switch to play the looped part. This probably says more about my ability than the looper. And in its defense a looper is quite simple, you just need to remember to push the button when you want to replay or to add a new part. I do like delay pedals, though. You just turn a few knobs to set it and press the button and there you go. Often, you may never have to mess with it again the entire night.

The second reason I am not afraid of AI is my thanks to drummers. In the era of scaling down because of economic pressures, many musicians are now playing as a single-act, or as a duo or trio. It becomes more difficult to belong to a large group of musicians, primarily because they like to be paid. I talk often with fellow musicians and the discussion sometimes moves to the idea of replacing other members with say a looper (see above) or replacing a drummer with a drum machine. Although using these technologies sounds like a workable idea, we fail to realize that these replacements often require previous and sometimes advanced programming before using them as part of the band. The beauty of working with real people is that you can look at each other, anticipate each other, and play off each other. With a machined device, you must work within the parameters set up by the programming thereby limiting the chance of improvisation that goes beyond the algorithm. These restrictions may be even more pronounced with drum machines. You can't look at a drum machine and subtly indicate that you want to change the beat, or the drum machine cannot "see you" and change from what it has been programmed to do–a real drummer can.

Although we may believe we are in competition with AI technology, we don't have to be. AI and humans may eventually co-exist but in some weird parallel universe. We still have the freedom to create in our own way regardless of advancements in AI. Of course, there are issues now and those that will arise such as copyright infringement and corporations using AI not to pay for the human artist's work. But keep in mind for those who remember that a more simple, analog versions of AI existed, and these were the "K-Tel" variety of vinyl records that presented performers who "played in the style of..."

After I finish writing this article, I will play my guitar having access to every transcription, notes, and chords of every song ever written. I can download millions of music and instructional videos from YouTube and other places. And maybe one day I will come across a music video by Bob and Tally! Or I may have the opportunity to play with AI generated "people." Do I feel connected to the universe? Or do I feel a creeping singularity? I don't know. But if we are on the cusp of technological singularity, I have no choice but to evolve and to understand my place in the AI universe. But for now, I am watching a music video and hoping that the buffering doesn't take too long.

* * *

Playing Well with Others: Moving Beyond the Groove

One of my favorite bands was Cream. The first album I ever bought as a teenager was Cream's *Disraeli Gears*. This album not only inspired me to play guitar, but I also heard the story that Eric Clapton learned guitar by confining himself to his room and did nothing but work on the guitar for two years. Now it has never been clear if this is a true story given his extensive early career playing, but I meagerly attempted something similar at age 14.

What I began to understand as I listened to this group is the intricate interplay that goes on between musicians and is particularly pronounced in a three-piece band, such as Cream. One of my favorite albums later was their live album *Live Cream* that included extended soloing by Clapton, along with the intricate interplay of Jack Bruce's bass, with Ginger Baker's jazz and rock licks. What struck me was that these extended works showed a communication among the three musicians that created a truly memorable recording. Although each was playing their own thing, the music itself became something greater than each members' contribution.

This interaction of the three musicians was something of a gestalt. From the creative input of each member the music went beyond each member, and transcended the bounds of meter, time, and musical space. Some would call it playing in the groove and certainly that would be the case here. Groove is an interesting concept as it can be used to define what happens when musicians are so in sync with each other that the only way to describe it is "being in the groove."

Attempts to describe what groove means is to use examples such as a feeling of swing, a shared feeling among members, an energetic force. Some descriptors are more profound such as a life force or heartbeat. Some suggest that it is like the music is playing itself, or that one is being pulled into a musical notch. A more technical, but somewhat vague description is that groove is a relationship between technique and feeling. We can talk about it as a chemistry, or a flow experience. But again, these are descriptions of the state.

We may know when it is that we are "in the groove," but what gets us there? Also, our presentation of the concept is broader in that we can understand it as a unit, a gestalt, as an implicit communication. We also can describe it as being outside ourselves–maybe we can even speak of it as something supernatural, or paranormal. As we create the music and become immersed in the experience of groove, it is something that arises from the music we create, it is a coming into a unique relationship with other members in the group, but it can also involve the listener who becomes part of the groove experience.

We can ask what gets us to this place we call groove? Some of the components that get us there are interpersonal. It is important to establish a rapport among all members of the group. Members talk to each other, engage in light conversation, and are particularly interested in each member as a person. Ultimately, I believe the key is to respect each other. Rapport, conversation, and respect make everyone comfortable to be there and to engage in the musical experience.

Another important component is developing one's musicianship. Musicianship as a way toward groove is to know the music and to have an appreciation of the genre. If you do not like the music, then you cannot respect it–you cannot groove. Communication is important. Here this involves musical communication. Listen to others. Although you may not be the soloist, do not become the center of attention. Listen to those playing around you and play off them. Listen to rhythm, timing, and feel; then enter into and become part of the communication. It is like being caught up in a stream of sound and experience–ride along with it.

Ultimately, we may not yet know what groove is, but we do know when we are in the groove. It moves us beyond ourselves and allows us to interact and relate to others in a special way. When we experience groove, we are in a place where music becomes that ultimate language that says things that we cannot say otherwise.

* * *

A Funny Thing Happened on the Way
to a Concert in the Park

Opportunity for new learning happens when we travel beyond the commonplace, either in our explicit actions and conscious thinking, or otherwise. It is in the unexpected that gives us a deeper insight into ourselves and what is possible as we seek to live adaptively and fully. Thus, in the slumber and revelry of a mid-summer dream, it was quite interesting to be swept up in a fantasy of a family outing, and the funny thing that happened on the way to a Concert in the park.

As my family and I entered the park, we noticed that a large crowd had gathered outside the amphitheater, and were making rhythmic drumming, shimmering rattles, and kazoo-like sounds. It was a great cacophony! As we got closer to the open-air theater we met the Band Director who offered us kazoos, a woodblock and mallet, or tambourine. She told us that they were now rehearsing for the concert's finale, entitled, "Oye Como Va" (trans., "Hey, how am I doing), which included audience participation. The band director further instructed that everyone would be able to play a part if they like, and that we should expect a rhumba line to form as people leave the amphitheater. Further, she invited us to take our musical instruments home with us to share with family and friends. It was another opportunity, the director suggested, that we could use music to celebrate our living. My family and I had a great time, and later as we reflected on our experience, we agreed that it was another example of how music affords us an opportunity to find delight in its sounds, to creatively express our feelings, to build bridges that connect people and communities, and to move past the anxious feelings and uncertainties of the moment.

As my dream suggests, the mind is boundless and unconstrained in its imaginative portrayal of our fantasies and desires. The mind is also often unrestrained in its presentation of unresolved conflicts and feelings, and their accompanying anxieties. But where does our anxiety come from? As the renowned existential therapist Irving Yalom proposes, the sources of our uneasiness arise from four existential concerns that we spend much of our time addressing and attempting to resolve: The most prominent is the uncertainty of our existence and the fleeting temporal characteristic of our lives. This basic concern leads us onto many different paths and ways of acting, always with the hope of securing our safety and personal survival. A second and associated concern we confront is our desire to live free and be self-determinate in our actions, so that we may find and experience the comforts and pleasures of life. A third concern extends our desire for comfort and pleasure to the interpersonal and communal levels, where we strive to form intimate and caring relationships with those in our family and others in our communities. The fourth concern implicitly incorporates all the others as it involves our unique personal identity and explanation regarding the purpose and meaning of our lives.

As we consider these existential issues, we recognize the power of music to aid us in meeting and addressing these concerns. As arts-therapist Natalie Rogers noted, music like other arts affords us a way to become aware of our feelings and thoughts, and to cathartically express them in our singing and dancing, drawing and painting, and in other creative expressions. These activities often lead us to a place of inner peace and balance. A place where we may find new hope and feel capable of greater compassion, sense a deeper understanding of other perspectives, and express a positive orientation for the next steps we take in our life's journey.

Thus, as expressed in my dream, what the band director in the park invited was for us to use music once again to take on and overcome the existential challenges we face. Reminding us that even though we may encounter uncertainty in our living, we also need to have fun and can be joyful in the present musical moment; to innovate and be free to express our feelings and ideas, in ways that only perhaps music allows us; to unite in harmony with others and find new connections with communities, and in unison to discover ways of addressing our collective concerns; and to sing out and announce ourselves, expressing our unique rhythm and dance of life.

As we travel beyond the commonplace, recognizing a newness and pleasure in our experience, we are reminded of our great potential to be creative–to express ourselves and tell our unique life-story as a musician, a painter, a dancer, a poet, a photographer, a sculptor, a writer, or creator of any other artistic, crafty, or imaginative thing. At any age, music and the arts provide us a way to take on the challenges of life, to find an explanation for the events and circumstances we meet, and to proclaim a hope for our future. Thus, like the Band Director from my mid-summer dream, we encourage the reader to take up a musical instrument, to break out pens and paint brushes, to sculpt, to knit and weave, to sing out, and dance to the melodies they hear so that we may join with one another in a celebration of life– expressing a compassion and unconditional regard for one another that will proclaim and leave a legacy of our hope, joy, and love.

* * *

The Circus

Standing on the high-wire is my job,
As I look down upon the endless mob,
Teetering and tottering amid shrieks and sobs–
I get paid. – It is my job.

The fat lady smiles as I do my set.
Her perfume is of whiskey and cigarettes.
She dreams of the ringmaster; he is her pet.
But his love grows smaller as the fatter she gets.

The clowns are running around the place
Tripping each other and giving chase–
All dressed up in their stripes and lace.
When the grease paint comes off–they have no face.

The animals are hungry and need to be fed.
The water boy is off somewhere dreaming in bed.
The spotlight and jugglers have gone to his head.
"I wanna be a star" is all he said.

We see the ringmaster as he takes off his hat.
"Thank you for coming. Hope you could see where
    you sat."
He looks for applause as he shakes his baby fat...
But the people are gone. They've seen enough of
    that.

The circus is over, and the tents come down.
The wagons creak with a "circus" sound.
I have to smile as I look around.
My life is a circus–my home's the next town.

* * *

Chapter 2 – Music as Metaphor

Music, in all its symbolisms and meanings, is a metaphor for life. It connects us to the common experiences we all share. And, through music we discover and learn more about ourselves, other people, and the world in which we live. Describing further how we might understand music, in the essay, "Softly, Gently, Music Casts its Spell," Dean notes that music dynamically portrays all human emotions. Indeed, music is a universal language that connects people and cultures. Again with much light-heartedness, Scott addresses the issue of copyright violations in "Who Stole the Kishka?" and how we can properly credit others for their work. When we make our deserted island lists, what are we really trying to do? In the essay, "They Call Me 'Guitar'," Scott addresses what it takes to have the epithet of "guitar" as part of your name and the exclusiveness of making lists. In the essays "Fifth Dimension" and "A Comedy of Errors," Dean proposes that in the complex aspects and sounds of music, the listener is the cohesive fifth dimension, and provides insight into the unique relationship that exists between comedy and music. Finally, Scott concludes the theme of music as metaphor in "I know One Note, and I am Going to Play It" by comparing playing a one note solo to the importance of making the one life you have count.

* * *

Softly, Gently, Music Casts Its Spell

In the libretto of Andrew Lloyd Webber's musical *The Phantom of the Opera*, the protagonist, born with facial disfigurement so severe that he hides his face behind a mask, describes the rapturous power of music to overcome and possess its listener in the story it tells. Conveying its tacit meaning, music moves us in a dream-like fashion to encounter ecstasy beyond our despair, peace beyond our inner agitation, and inspiration that compels and moves us to deeper reflection and action. Thus, music, in all the ways we may interact with it (e.g., composing, listening, moving to, playing), has been suggested to bring an inner solace and comfort, and used to aid and induce relaxation, to become psychologically or spiritually centered, and as a technique to assist in recovery and healing processes. So, let's explore how music casts its spell.

How Music Casts Its Spell: An Aural-Neural Conversation

Engaging the listener in an aural-neural conversation of sorts, the rhythms of music vigorously innervates and entrains neural systems of the brain. Neural entrainment refers to a synchronization of brain waves that affects our cognitive and physical responses. For example, we may walk faster or exercise more vigorously, or work and process information more quickly, as we listen to energetic music whose fast tempos and strong beats direct us to keep up with the pace. Further, music may distract us from feelings of discomfort or fatigue, allowing us to walk, exercise, or work longer. Music may also affect our mood, especially if the music elicits the production and release of hormones which are related to feelings of pleasure and relaxation (e.g., dopamine, endorphins, serotonin, and oxytocin).

Looking closer and considering the dynamic characteristics of a piece of Western music, we discover its emotional tone (e.g., agitation, comfort, excitement, relief) conveyed through its orientation in a major or minor key, the upward or downward direction of the melody as it moves along the musical scale, its tempo or speed and moments of moving faster (allegro) or slower (adagio), the accenting of particular rhythmic beats, the sounding of many notes on a single beat (e.g., triplets) or sustaining a single tone for many beats, as well as by changing from soft (piano) to loud (forte), and adding different instruments or voices to the musical conversation. For example, when we ask how music is used to induce a state of mind-body relaxation, we find that music composed in Major keys that also have a slow tempo (andante), and a low amplitude of sound (piano) are reported to produce calming effects. We may also call to mind Gioachino Rossini's orchestral work the "William Tell Overture," where a musical story is told through the introduction of different melodic themes which are relaxed and gentle, or race up or down the musical scale. Further, emotional color is expressed throughout Rossini's overture via harmonic modulation from major to minor keys, contrasts between the soft and gentle sounds of the strings and woodwinds, along with gallant and heroic sounds of the brass and percussion instruments, and shifts in tempo from adagio (slow) to allegro (fast). Examining the overture's four sections, the "Prelude" is set in the key of E-Major and begins with slow and gentle sounds of the strings. The following section, "Storm," set in the key of E-Minor communicates an emotional agitation voiced by the woodwinds and brass. Later, the section "Ranz des Vaches," set in the key of E-Major, intimates the calm after the storm with soft strings and comforting oboe, flutes, and horn. The overture's "Finale," is set in the key of E-Major and opens with trumpet and trombone fanfares, followed by the strings and full orchestra which sounds like horses galloping, heralding a regal ending. The "Finale's" key musical motif is quite recognizable to many of us kids growing up in 1950s and 1960s, as it was used as the theme for the television show *The Lone Ranger*.

How Music Casts Its Spell: Cultural and Communal Connections

When we consider music from cultural and communal perspectives, we recognize that it is a universal language that allows us to make connections with people from many different backgrounds and world-views, and to express and explore our deepest feelings and most pressing concerns. In many ways, music invites us to step beyond our own ego-centric concerns. To share and unite with others and to join in cultural practices and communal causes. For example, inducing feelings of awe in its musical expression, Hussein Janmohamed's choral work, "Rise Children, Rise to Peace," communicates a message that asks the listener to compassionately embrace the dignity of each person, to seek social justice, and to strive for peace. Perhaps, in ways other musical instruments cannot, the human voice is recognized to be especially effective at conveying cultural and communal messages, due to its very wide emotional range and tonal color, and our neurological sensitivity to extract meaning from its acoustic sounds and linguistic expressions.

All aspects of human emotion and expression are also found in the sounds of the drum, rattle, cymbals and gongs, whistles, and stringed instruments. Noting that there are no-borders or geographical restrictions in music, the percussion and stringed instruments from all continents have become featured musical voices in jazz and symphony orchestras throughout the world. For example, Kumi-daiko, the art of Japanese drumming, comparable to idiomatic expressions found in jazz, uses very rich and different rhythmic patterns to reflect both the wide range of human emotions (e.g., excited, explosive, entranced, relaxed, tranquil) as well as the tempos of nature.

A related percussive ensemble and musical art form, the gamelan, is found in Malaysia, Indonesia, and Singapore. The percussion instruments used include a set of tuned brass plates or gongs of various sizes. In contrast to the major and minor modalities of Western music, the gamelan is usually tuned to a five-note scale (e.g., C, D-flat, E-flat, G, A-flat, C), and its sound is somewhat to that of the glockenspiel, marimba or xylophone. The gamelan orchestra is comprised of a range of low- and high-pitched instruments, that may also include drums, flutes, and stringed instruments. Gamelan music, while uniquely a cultural art form of the Malay people, celebrates the universal ideals of cohesiveness and cooperation, human and mythological drama, and representations of the cosmic that we find in music throughout the world.

Like the drum and rattle, the flute is played in all cultures and is one of the oldest instruments. It expresses a melodic voice that is capable of being soft and airy, poetic and venerable, warm and ethereal, as well as penetratingly sharp and shrill. It may portray the sound of bird songs, the whistling wind, as well as other sounds of nature. Further, in its soft and warm tonal color, the sound of the flute is recognized as calming and relaxing, and used by First Nations and Indigenous Peoples as part of their sacred healing ceremonies. Thus, the flute's soft expressions invoke deep inner reflection, and its shrill chirps may bring forth a new sense of connecting with nature or a transcendence beyond oneself.

In India, the sitar, a plucked stringed instrument is used in Hindi song and Indian classical music. The sitar may contain 18 to 21 strings, with five primary strings that are used for the melody, drone strings that sound a counterpoint to the melodic strings, and sympathetic strings that are not plucked but sound in sympathy with the other strings. The term "raga" refers to a musical form designed to allow boundless improvisation, and where the musical intention is to affect the deepest emotions and aspects of mind. This musical art form uses rhythmic drumming and plucked stringed harmonies to support embellished chthonian-like melodies that express universal concerns.

Similarly, in the acoustic guitar we encounter polyphonic experiences that may convey the excitement and gravity of our deepest concerns and personal intimacies. The guitar's gentle bell-like harmonics also invite us into a deeper reflection and meditative contemplation, and its strummed and arpeggiated chords may portray the gentleness of a flowing river or the tumult of cascading rapids. In a related way, the sounds of the rhythm and blues guitar may invigorate and serve as a balm for life's struggles. Taking up deeply felt and soulful concerns, blues music through its very accented and shifting rhythms, bending of tones, and use of a pentatonic scale plus one added note, may affect us to our deepest core. Rhythm and Blues has universal appeal and is the root from which various styles of funk, hip-hop, and rock have originated.

Living Again Beyond the Mask

Music's therapeutic effects may allow us to be expressive of our emotions in new ways and live beyond the social camouflage of one's mask, communicating and revealing our true identity. For example, in an integrative arts therapy program, an older man with dementia was observed adjusting his style of painting based on the type of music that was played: When upbeat jazz was played he painted with bolder colors; lighter and more fluid colors were used when painting to classical music; and softer music encouraged a calmer painting process. In a related manner, in music therapy research where nursing home residents listened to their favorite music on headphones, music listening was suggested to positively enhance emotional state and social behaviors, and decrease need for psychotropic medicines. In other research, listening to personalized music playlists was suggested to improve quality of life for dementia patients, while also improving personal relationships with and reducing stress for their caregivers.

Certainly, like the Phantom, we recognize the power of music to overtake us with excitement and elation, to provide us comfort and relaxation, and to inspire us as we meet the challenges of everyday living. In its melodies, rhythms, and harmonies, we find expression of our deepest emotions and the language of personal transformation and social change. Thus, let us give way to music's power to instill inner peace or move us to ecstasy, and realize in music a restoration of our inner balance and communal harmony.

* * *

Who Stole the Kishka? The Copyright Problem in Music

I was listening to Frankie Yankovic's popular recording of the polka "Who Stole the Kishka?" Because of its lively polka beat and infectious lyrics, it is often played at wedding receptions, and to close a show. I wonder what makes this popular song so enjoyable, not only to polka-holics, but to myself, a mere polka-imbiber? Is it the lyrics, the beat? Or as participants in the old *Bandstand* program rated popular songs of the day: "I give it an 85, you can dance to it." Now of course polka music is the type of music that gets folks dancing. As well, people enjoy singing the lyrics of this song and especially the last line imploring the thief to bring it back. Maybe what makes it popular is that you can insert anyone's name into the lyrics as to who the suspect might be and who found it. However, listening to it this time got me thinking about the lyrics and perhaps there is a broader implication to those words than just documenting the theft of a sausage. In fact, I thought about how this song is an interesting allegory to describe copyright violations and the theft of another's artistic work. Who they might be, and can they bring it back?

The most recent case of an alleged violation of copyright was one claiming that Ed Sheeran's song "Thinking Out Loud" was a rendition of Marvin Gayes's "Let's Get it On." After a lengthy battle, the court exonerated Ed Sheeran finding that he did not plagiarize the song. Another case of copyright violation was when the Rachmaninov estate contacted the singer, songwriter, Eric Carmen about a possible copyright infringement of Rachmaninov's *Piano Concerto No. 2.* Both agreed on a settlement where Carmen gave song-writing credit for "All by Myself" to Rachmaninov with the estate receiving 12 percent royalties from the sales. According to Eric Carmen, at the time he wrote the song, he believed the piano concerto was in the public domain.

Although many songs have borrowed melodies or themes from other songs, typically these borrowings have been from music that no longer is protected by copyright laws. Many classical pieces could be considered outside copyright, but this too is not so clear as these rights might be held by an estate, as in Eric Carmen's example, or although the composition itself is no longer copyrighted, the recordings, production, or sheet music may be.

To understand copyright law is to engage in an angst-ridden, mind-numbing, brain-splitting enterprise. Even though most songwriters, performers, and writers engage in a diligent review of their sources to insure against plagiarism, lost hours of sleep can be attributed to wondering if one will be "called out" for using the work of another. One safeguard (although no less complicated) is to always acknowledge the work of another from whom you have borrowed, that is, to acknowledge the source. Some acts of borrowing without citing are explicit, some are inadvertent, innocent, or due to ignorance in that the person was unaware that they had used someone else's already published idea or believed that it no longer was a copyrighted piece. Regardless, copyright battles affect one's reputation whether rightfully or wrongfully so. And reputation once damaged can take a long time to repair.

The problem of copyright is further complicated with the rise of APPs that detect plagiarism. In the early days, these APPs such as *Turnitin* could be used to detect if a student was using the works of another without appropriate references. Now, in principle a possibly useful tool; however, not so easy in practice. The APP would indicate that a part of the work was plagiarized because it considered the actual citations the writer used in their paper to be evidence of plagiarism–the irony is not lost in that the writer included their sources to ensure that they were not plagiarizing the work of another! Of course, most instructors understood that this was a potential flaw in the system and adjusted accordingly, but it is disconcerting to the hapless student to see the APP accuse them that their paper was 95% the work of another! Some attest that with the proper safeguards and "enlightenment" the APP could be usefully applied. I always believed however, that if one considered themselves to be an expert in their field, that they should have a firm grasp of the literature and be able to detect on their own any evidence of direct plagiarism or if a student paper seemed a bit "off" or too well written warranting further scrutiny. Although some students will try to bend the rules, in my experience these attempts are quite transparent and unsophisticated. I even had a student turn in a paper written by his girlfriend who took my class the previous year but forgot to remove her name from the paper! However, the problem has become more compounded by more advanced plagiarism that is becoming harder to detect without APP "police" to check and detect AI generated works. And I am confident that even a "blindfolded" AI pounding away at a virtual keyboard will eventually "steal" lines from a well-known piece of music, art, or writing.

I am waiting for the revisit of the Eric Carmen incident when AI is asked to create something in the style of Rachmaninov, and it presents to the listener a song by Eric Carmen! Perhaps the most we could ask for from AI is that somehow it notifies the listener, reader, or watcher that this is an AI-generated product. If AI is a disinterested, non-emotional entity, then it should feel no slight if it must within its programming recognize and report that it is AI produced and that it is its human handlers who are the ones gaining any profit from its work–a weird type of exploitation indeed!

Perhaps citing one's sources or who and what inspired your creation could be applied to all artistic endeavors, whether it be writing, creating art such as painting, sculpting, or music. Citing one's source in a piece of writing is a customary practice. It is usually found within the text, or as footnotes, or end notes. It has been suggested that a way to cite one's sources can be found and implemented in other artistic works, as well. For example, in music, a list of sources that inspired the work could be listed below the song, or on the cover of the LP, or CD, or on a platform such as YouTube, or Spotify.

When writing a piece of music, I would conclude that the best way to cite your source is to include it right in the song. The band Steppenwolf has done this brilliantly in their song "Tighten up your Wig." The song is a direct borrowing of Junior Wells' "Messin' with the Kid." In the song John Kay in a tribute to the blues man, acknowledges in the lyrics that they, indeed, stole the song from him. Perhaps if we all acknowledged those we are indebted to, the world would be a better place.

* * *

They Call Me "Guitar"

We all like to make our deserted island lists. It could be a list of your favorite books, albums or CDs (provided electricity or internet access is available on your island). If you were asked to make a deserted island list of your favorite guitar players, we would likely have our own personal favorites but certainly there would be many overlapping examples. It seems evident when we see the list of the top 100, 75, or 10 guitar players of all time that these lists would be very similar. Not to take anything away from these players as I am a mere mortal guitar picker among these "gods who have walked the earth," I do want to point out, and I am safe to say that not one of them on these lists sport the moniker "Guitar" as part of their name.

It takes a rare person to apply to themselves or be given by others the title "Guitar." To me it implies you are the defining voice for that instrument. It also means that you better be able to deliver "the goods" when you play. I would like to present three examples who, indeed, are deserving of the name "Guitar."

Beverly "Guitar" Watkins

Beverly "Guitar" Watkins was born on April 6, 1939, in Atlanta, GA and died at 80 years of age on October 1, 2019. Although she began playing as a youngster in high school, it wasn't until the age of 60 when she delivered her first solo album. With her infectious smile and hard driving attack, she was an unsung innovator of guitar playing. Often seen playing the guitar behind her back (much in the style of Jimi Hendrix), or on her knees and leaning way back, she delivered a master class in "rock attitude" and full-on blues. When asked how she learned to play like she did, she replied, "Jesus." Six months before her death, with her throaty-voiced blues and Fender in hand she demonstrated why she deserved the title "Guitar." I recommend listening to examples of her playing on YouTube. Of joy to watch is when she played at the Foundry, in Athens, Ga with the Rick Fowler Band. Her rendition of "Sweet Home Chicago" will send chills up your spine and put a smile on your face.

Johnny "Guitar" Watson

Johnny "Guitar" Watson was the original "Gangster of Love." His guitar playing was a joyous mix of classic blues and funk. He could put the funk in the bucket and take it back out again. A consummate stage performer, and superb on harp and keyboards. One of the top 3 guitar players on Frank Zappa's list. Born on February 3, 1935. He died May 17, 1996, while on stage in Yokohama Japan of a heart attack at the age of 61.

"Guitar" Slim

Even better is to have "Guitar" as your first name. Guitar Slim (Eddie Jones) was born in Greenwood, MS on December 10, 1926. His signature song, "The Things I Used to Do" was recorded by Stevie Ray Vaughn, Albert Collins, The Fabulous Thunderbirds, and many more, and is a must play among all blues bands. He died of pneumonia on February 7, 1959, at the age of 32.

Revisiting Our Deserted Island List

An unfortunate artifact of these top guitar player lists, whether it be pop, rock, jazz, or blues is that they are predominantly male. Although female and transgender guitar players can be found on these lists, they are relatively few. We should highlight that constructing lists of all-time guitarists that are predominantly male is an anachronism of the cultural construct of gender. And unfortunately, status and rank were determined along gender lines and still is very much today. Why is it that female guitarists have often been looked on as second-class citizens of the guitar? I will leave the social problem of gender and guitar to those who have greater skill and legitimacy to analyze this issue than me. However, I would like the reader to consider an alternative top list of guitar players to include on their deserted island list that is free from gender designators.

The above three I mentioned should be a start. But also consider the following:

> Mary Kaye (Malia Ka'aihue). Considered "the first lady of rock and roll." She had her own Fender Stratocaster named after her.

> Carol Kaye. One of the most prolific bassists in history. A gifted artist and studio musician, her bass is featured on numerous recordings from the 1960s Golden Era of pop and rock and roll music hit records.

> Hazel Dickens. Activist for coal miners. Her songs such as "Black Lung" and "Coal Mining Women" spoke of the hardships of mining on workers and families and the injustice and inequity perpetrated by coal companies.

Here are more guitarists to consider that you can easily look up:

Barbara Lynn
Etta Baker
Mary Osborne
Lari Basilio
Ana Popovic
Orianthi
Pasquale Grasso
St. Vincent
Bireli Lagrene
Emily Remler
Dylana Nova Scott
Roy Clark
Susan Tedeschi
Mabel Carter
Laura Jane Grace
Leslie Mariah Andrews

It seems that our list is getting ever longer. As much fun as they are to make, I suggest that maybe it is time to throw away the lists. Lists are inherently exclusionary as someone will always be left out. Besides, how likely is it that any of us will be stuck on a deserted island anyway? Instead let's take advantage of the unlimited access we have today to hear many more guitarists than ever before. It sure beats sitting on a deserted island and drawing a face on a coconut for company!

* * *

The Fifth Dimension

In terms of its most basic physical characteristics, sound is a pressure wave moving through space. Thus, as a wave form, sound is recognized to have four dimensions: amplitude, pitch, timbre, and time. Amplitude refers to the measurable height of the sound wave. Smaller sound waves, like the gentle ripples produced when a pebble is thrown into a pool of water, reflect soft and whispering sounds. Correspondingly, large sound waves, like the much bigger waves that are produced when a large stone is cast into the water, reflect loud and roaring sounds. Pitch is a function of the distance between the peaks of each sound wave. High pitched sounds have a shorter distance between the peaks of each wave. In contrast, low pitch sounds have longer distances between the sound wave peaks. Timbre refers to the tone quality or color of sound. Different musical instruments and each person's voice have their own timbre. In terms of its physical characterization, timbre refers to the particular shape of the sound wave and the unique overtone series or additional sound wave characteristics that are produced by a particular musical instrument or by a particular voice. For example, some instruments, like voices, sound brassy and boisterous. Other instruments and voices, sound nasal and penetrating. The production and movement of the wave through space represents the fourth dimension of time.

These physical characteristics, however, are not enough to understand how sound, and more importantly, how music may be perceived and understood. Is there a fifth dimension then? Well, reasoning with tongue firmly implanted in cheek, yes, there is a musical group called "The 5th Dimension."

But more to the point, is there a possible fifth dimension to sound? And if so what might it be? Well from a psychological perspective we should note that all the characteristics of sounds noted above reflect merely physical properties of the sound wave. For us to discern these dimensions, and more accurately, perceive the sound as music or the sonorous voice of a close and dear friend, requires a psychoacoustic analysis that distinguishes music from noise and language sounds. Further, like language, to make the sounds interpretable as music, with its simple or eloquent conveyance of emotional expression, requires a further mixing and analytic filtering that takes into account repeated aspects of the sound waves, as well as melodic and harmonic features. Interesting, like the dynamic and multiple characteristic features of language, the sounds of music are also perceived and interpreted differently.

Indeed, as Stefanos Iakovides and colleagues report, music is perceived differently by normal subjects and psychiatric patients, and thus conceptualized as conveying different emotions via the musical experience. Moreover, in combination with age-associated changes in hearing and sensory-perceptual functioning, there are also reports suggesting age-variation in the perceived loudness of a musical excerpt, perception of the sounds of speech, as well as in neural-cognitive processing of harmonic tonal perceptions in the auditory cortex region of the brain.

Embracing a psychoacoustic orientation, where the physical characteristics of sound are in dynamic relation to our perceptual experience, we propose that an additional characteristic of sound is the listener. In doing so we suggest the person's cultural background, personality, musical preferences, and ways of seeing themselves influence how one may "hear" and experience music. Thus, the fifth dimension of sound is the listener and their personal interaction with the other auditory characteristics that produce the phenomenological reality we create, impose, and discover in our musical experiences. Yet, as noted in a review by Kim Armstrong, in all cultures, and for all people, there is a noted "sameness" or similarity in how we may categorize music as pastoral and sacred, or exciting and inspiring us to dance, or as expressions of the deep emotions of love or loss, or as relaxing and calming like a lullaby that is conducive to sleep.

Understanding the person as an essential component of the musical experience, as the fifth dimension, informs us as to why some folks prefer or dislike certain styles of music. Moreover, this recognition leads us into a deeper reflection about what the music means, where we may more aptly discern its symbolisms, those ideas and qualities that the sounds of music portray and express. As alluded in the popular song by the Kiki Dee Band, "I've Got the Music in Me," music is a "part" us. As we listen it innervates the cognitive and affective areas of our brains, instilling thoughts, moderating our mood, and compelling us to action. Thus, we may deepen our experience with music as we seek to understand how our favorite songs and symphonies may be enjoyable, insightful, or restful. And, concomitantly, in our deeper analysis of music, come to know ourselves in a more profound way.

* * *

A Comedy of Errors

Music is everywhere if we listen. Indeed, we find the sounds of music and its unique expressions throughout the natural and our human-made environments. Within the natural world, we hear music in the howling winds of a great tempest, the rustling of leaves in a gentle breeze, and the chirps, squawks, shrieks, and snarls of animal communications heard in the wild. In the human-made world, the rat-a-tat-tat noise of the jackhammer, the beeps, honks and roars of rush-hour traffic, the sirens of firetrucks, and the chiming of church bells offer themselves as musical expressions as well. Also recognized in this human-made domain are the more formal compositional areas of orchestral music and other contemporary works intended to portray both nature and to express intimate human and social concerns, as well as the distinctive category blurring of "noise music," a musical genre that uses electronic sounds in an expressive, musical way. Without doubt then, music, often communicating ideas and feelings that cannot be expressed in other ways, is everywhere if we care to listen!

So, it is quite interesting to consider music as an expression of our humorous and amusing human experiences. Perhaps the best examples of music's ability to express comedy and facetious life portrayals are in the musical-comedy acts of yesteryear, like those of Victor Borge and Spike Jones, or the more contemporary sounds of Weird Al Yankovic and others. Always at the edge of the absurd, these accomplished performers use music to help us laugh at our human condition, and in turn have thrilled and entertained audiences of all ages.

Victor Borge, a child prodigy and concert pianist with great virtuosic flare, could never be serious about the serious music he performed. Instead, throughout his career he would interrupt his playing with satirical humor, deadpan jokes, and clever wordplay to offer his audience something to laugh about. He was serious about being unserious!

Spike Jones was a band leader and conductor who with his band offered spoofs on many of the hits of the day. Touring North America with his band in the 1940s and 1950s as "The Musical Depreciation Revue," Spike introduced an array of "never-heard-before" musical instruments, like the "birdaphone" (a rubber-band powered instrument that produced a "brr-ing" raspberry sound), fog-horns, and the "latrinophone" (a toilet seat with playable strings), used in innovative musical arrangements that incorporated sounds not usually associated with band music–like sirens, car-crashes, whistles, burps, hiccups and gunshots to allow for levity and humor–much to the pleasure and excitement of the audience.

Weird Al Yankovic, starting with his name, intentionally seeks to evoke laughter and merry making. His parodies of rock and popular hits always meet the musical standards of the original, yet his outlandish shifting of lyrics ingeniously introduces and tells an absurd story. For example, a parody of Michael Jackson's "Beat It" becomes "Eat It," as the lyrics shift from a young person's embracing an identity of being "tough" and "bad," to the young person's concern refocused on food. It may have just sounded bizarre and off-center–but that's Weird Al–calling attention to the parodies inherent "weirdness" to make people laugh.

Comicality is also recognized in many musical burlesque acts and revues, where music is intertwined with fun-making and at times profane lampooning, as exemplified in the musical fantasy and comedy movie *Tenacious D in the Pick of Destiny*, directed by Liam Lynch and starring Jack Black and Kyle Gass. With similar lighthearted intent, jazz musicians in their improvisation are also well known for inserting a phrase such as "Pop Goes the Weasel," "Mary Had a Little Lamb," or the "Popeye" theme into their solos, not only to demonstrate their proficiency and command of the music, but also to include a bit of levity into their music making.

But why do we find humor in music? Well first, let's consider what humor might be. Early on, humor and its associated laughter, was thought by the Greek philosopher Aristotle to express a superiority over other people and their circumstances, or of a former state of ourselves. Later philosophical thought suggested humor and laughter as a pressure-release device of our nervous system, used to relieve repressed feelings and nervous energies. A more recent philosophical explanation is that humor is a product of logical incongruities that we come upon; suggesting our amusement and laughter is a response to something that is beyond our expectations or usual patterns of thinking. These explanations for humor may all be sounding a bit "funny" to the reader, and you may be asking, "But, how does comedy and music go together?" Well, perhaps the easiest answer is that music may also express the sounds of fun and laughter! But in many ways, as the great conductor and composer Leonard Bernstein notes, humor in music is not just telling jokes about itself. What we find to be "funny," is funny for musical reasons. Humor in music is created through farcical contrasts and fluctuations, as well as abrupt changes and unexpected resolutions.

Nevertheless, what we find humorous in music, as Aristotle suggested, may be based on the funny recollection of what we might have sounded like when we were first a beginner, playing with starts-and-stops and other variations in tempo, and adding or including alternative notes in playing a melody or chord. Or, in accord with the release of nervous energies explanation, we might laugh when we hear a musical work that expresses an imposing mood of pomp and circumstance, as the sound may innervate, and thereby release suppressed emotions. Further, and closer to the reasoning offered by Maestro Bernstein, we laugh and find merriment in the unexpected musical incongruities that we hear. Like the amusement we may feel when we hear an off-key rendition, or a melodic or lyrical deviation of a well-known musical piece like "The Star-Spangled Banner" or "Happy Birthday."

Thus, humor offers us a way to feel superior to how we might have been at a moment earlier in our life, or find release of pent-up psychical tension, or be amused by the illogical or incongruous nature of what is being expressed. Whether it is when Victor Borge's stops playing "Tea for Two" to offer a funny insight about the keys on the piano, or Spike Jones' introduction of the unexpected realism of sound-effects and satirical singing within a song like "Wyatt Earp Makes Me Burp," the musical joke makes us laugh. And in our laughter, we may discover a way to re-balance our current life concerns and find a new inner harmony.

Indeed it is well noted that humor is good for our health. If we can laugh–even at ourselves–somehow in the funny juxtaposition of the logical and illogical, there is a release of neurochemicals associated with pleasure and positive emotions (e.g., dopamine, endorphins), and we find the all-too-seriousness of the world not as difficult to deal with. Further, when we laugh, we discover something about ourselves. Laughter is a coping mechanism that releases an inner tension, allowing us to be, for a moment at least, more emboldened so that a challenge like a health problem that we may be apprehensive about, becomes less onerous to manage. In truth, laughter is a great remedy for many of the things that ail us.

Oh, and that reminds me of a joke: At the weekly community band practice recently, a person walked up to the band director and asked about joining the band. The director said, "Great! You can join the trombone section!" The person, a bit flustered, replied, "But I play flute... I don't know how to play trombone!" "Well..." the director responded, "...that hasn't stopped anyone else!"

* * *

I Know One Note, and I'm Going to Play It!

Vinny Mazetta on the recording "Jones Girl," played a one note solo, a bit out of rhythm and a bit out of tune throughout. It has been described as quite awful and the worst solo ever recorded. Keep in mind though, that this example was an alternate take not used on the final recording—but that one too is a bit off as well. This example can also illustrate the awfulness of "oneness" when we think about phrases such as one-hit wonder, one-trick pony, or as the song by the group Three Dog Night implies, "one" is indeed a lonely experience. And as this essay will present, playing a solo is a difficult thing to do.

However, excellent one-note solos exist. Adam Neely on his YouTube channel presents examples of one note playing by saxophonist Big Jay McNeely ("Deacon's Hop"), guitarist Pete Townsend ("I Can See for Miles"), and Neil Young ("Cinnamon Girl"). In these songs, the solo although only one note, somehow interacts with other elements of the music in a way that moves the solo from something potentially monotonous to something inspired.

We propose that one-note playing can be a metaphor to living just one life. What does it mean to live having just one life? If we compare the one life we have to one-note playing, the bad elements that throw us out of sync with others and ourselves are those where we lose control and the direction of our lives. We live without intentionality or purpose. Another example, using a music analogy is that in our soloing our intonation is off. Intonation simply is playing in tune. Our instrument not only needs to be in tune, but we also need to be in tune with other musicians when we play. In life, we need to play or be in tune with ourselves and be in tune with how we interact with others. Soloing is making a statement of importance. And in life we must confront the question of whether our lives do not say much or do our lives say a lot.

Music can be thought of as a metaphor for life. We think of living our lives in harmony with ourselves, others, and society. We are one note built around the notes of many others. Even when we experience harmonic dissonance in life, it too as in music can resolve itself if we let it. We also think of the concept of Rhythm. Rhythm is how we move through life. Jimmy Bruno, the renowned jazz guitarist, is attributed to saying that western music has 12 notes, but it is rhythm that provides it with infinite possibilities. We understand that the rhythm of our life can hold many different beats, timing, and meter. The song "One Note Samba," by Antonio Carlos Jobim is an example of rhythm and movement. Although the first part of the song plays one note for the melody, it is the rhythm of the samba that gives it life. We also hear that over the one note melody, the chords are in constant movement. Thus, our lives can be filled with a smooth, flowing rhythm and graceful movement or a disruptive and disjointed thrashing about. Finally, melody is how we personally experience the world. Melody is in the statements we make, the actions we take, and our contact with others. We can live disharmoniously, in constant conflict with ourselves, others, and society. We may feel removed from life, that somehow, we are out of step, out of sync, not in rhythm with the flow of life. And indeed, when we play our personal melody or solo, we can be playing the music of our life beautifully, or simply playing an awful one-note solo.

We can play our one-note solo, not out of monotony or boredom, but one that is inspired. We can do that by always being curious, being creative, and always finding something interesting in our lives and the lives of others. We realize that life is a gift that provides interesting experiences. We can think about going with the rhythm of life, not constantly pushing against or seemingly to fight life all the time, but to understand that we live in a flow of experience, some good some bad. The key is to recognize the impermanence of these experiences and thus we can continue to move forward. Live your life with purpose and effect. Show that you are committed to life and to others who are important to you. Demonstrate that you want to leave something of you behind or pay it forward as the saying goes. Live your life with integrity and in harmony with others. If you know how to play only one note, play it boldly. Make your life a statement and a testament to others that they too have an important song to play.

* * *

Chapter 3 – Individual and Community Justice

As little children, many of us released a tearful emotional response when we fell and scraped our knee on the sidewalk, or felt someone hurt our feelings. And even though we may have been taught to "treat others the way we would like to be treated," it wasn't perhaps until later in adolescence when we could really understand and consider more deeply how other folks might think and feel. Taking up important social concerns that focus on how we treat one another, the first two essays of this chapter address the importance of recognizing and respecting the dignity of all persons. Scott, in the essay "Members Only," discusses our need for communal connection and our sense of belonging, and how our need to belong may be satisfied by others and even by ourselves. Our self-esteem can be undermined when others deny the importance of our work by trivializing it and this is the subject of Scott's essay "I Could do Your Job." The problems of social and community justice are taken up in the next three essays. How we can become desensitized to another's plight is the subject of Scott's essay "Although They May be Painful..." The concerns of social and community justice are also addressed by Dean in the dystopian essay "Seems Like 1984 has Come Early." Finally, Dean, in "How Do We Define a Well Society?" offers a prescription for how we can move toward treating each other with care and respect.

* * *

Members Only

The comedian Groucho Marx quipped "I would not want to be in a club that would have me as a member." However, the need to belong is a strong desire in all of us. It is cited as an important motivation in many psychological models. We go to great lengths to find acceptance and to feel a sense that we belong to something. For example, a long period of education, certification, or training is the currency to become a member of a profession or vocation. Once the dues are paid through hard work, we should expect acceptance by other members and to reap the benefits of being "in the club."

It only takes a cursory read of history to know that often this is not the case. Whether through racial, sexual, or status discrimination many are barred from membership, even when the dues were paid. We also know how important acceptance from others is because one of the greatest punishments by many societies and organizations is to bar, expel, exile, shun, or ostracize its members for perceived wrongdoing. It is a hard thing to be outside looking in. Now the question becomes, how much effort should one spend on trying to be part of a club before writing it off as a bad adventure no longer worthy of one's time?

Often acceptance into a profession or club is not the endpoint. There are further hoops and barrels one must go through not only to continue to attain full membership (e.g., the promotion process), but also performance expectations to keep membership. The dues paying never ends. And if you discontinue to walk the dues paying treadmill, you are likely then given the designation "dead wood" and risk shunning and possible expulsion. Now of course, if you are an accepted member of the club, these requirements are probably not an issue, and you may even believe they are a necessary part of membership. It may be that you feel some privileged status or that hard work was your entry. The problem with these two beliefs is that one may result in disdain of new members who are perceived to be "bucking the status quo" of privilege; the other is the belief that new members somehow did not work hard enough to be there.

We can also be our own worst enemy when we assess whether we are worthy of membership. All too often, we hear people who engage in what psychologists call the "impostor effect." This effect, or syndrome, is quite common, but insidious because the person believes that they are a fraud, experience high anxiety, and fear that they will be "found out" by their peers and associates. Although highly competent and successful, they still think that they are not worthy of belonging in "the club."

Several points can now be made regarding trying to be part of a club, profession, or organization:

> Point 1: Don't waste your time if it becomes clear that others will not accept you as a member. It is hard to walk away particularly if one has invested time and effort. The need to stay in the club becomes a "sunk cost" where one cannot leave because of how much has already been invested into trying to stay. It's like staying to the end of a bad movie simply because you paid for a ticket or determining to finish reading a terrible book because you have already invested time reading the first few chapters. The

idea of sunk cost is like throwing one's money, effort, or time into a lost cause. The more money, time, and effort you spend the harder it is to recognize that it is lost and harder to walk away.

Point 2: You find that after a deep examination of your goals and why you want to belong are in contrast with the membership expectations. Also, our expectations and reasons why we want to belong to something change over time. Perhaps your goals change or the outlook or mission of the organization changes.

Point 3: You find that you can attain your goals without being in the club. Perhaps going freelance or starting your own business or organization is the most desirable. Or, possibly finding another group of people who accept who you are.

But keep in mind before you decide to leave a group, that your acceptance was usually the outcome of a long vetting process and that you are likely the best candidate for admittance. Thus, do not feel like an impostor or interloper–you are not! Also, do not let the explicit or implicit faults of the organization, whether through its history (i.e., having only white males as CEO, or only male guitarists in rock bands), or interrelationship dynamics or personal agendas, trigger self-doubt or feelings of inadequacy. Who knows, you might be the one who changes the system! If you believe in yourself and believe this is the place for you and you believe you are the best person for membership, then do not let anything or anyone stop you. You will then be free psychologically and emotionally and ultimately gain the freedom to create and make changes on your own terms.

* * *

I Could Do Your Job

Maybe this has never happened to you, but some of us may have experienced an encounter where someone for whatever reason says, "this looks easy, I could do your job." There is a lot to parse out from this exhortation. One is that the person truly believes that they could do your job. They could have acquired the skill, training or education to do it. Or they believe it is so easy, that anyone could do it without any training, education, or skill at all. Or they're just having a bad day or are frustrated and unhappy and want to take it out on you.

I wish to explore why it is that many things are not as easy as they seem and why not everyone can do those things, and why people believe that they are easy. The underlying themes are the "illusion of ease" and a misunderstanding of what it means to become an expert at something.

My only experience with plumbing ended in disaster. How hard could it be to replace a shower knob. You just get a set of channel locks and twist off the old knob and then twist on the new knob. Well, if you forget to turn off the water before-hand, the water pressure shoots the knob to the other side of the shower with a clang and puts a big chip in the tile. Also, the water thoroughly soaked me before I could get to the shut off valve in the basement. I've also learned never to go near any project involving electricity!

Let's look at how this "illusion of ease" is created and how it contributes to the perception that a job is easy to do. An example where we often hear the statement "I could do your job," is in academia. Now some people I am sure believe that all a college professor does is stand up in front of a class and b.s. for

50 minutes and then goes to the office for an afternoon nap. (Maybe some do. I guess there is always a kernel of truth in any myth or stereotype). We particularly see this myth reinforced in mystery sitcoms and movies where the "professor" solves criminal cases AND conducts a full schedule of teaching, writing, researching, office hours, and administrative committee work! Thus, how hard can it be to stand up in front of a classroom and b.s. for 50 minutes? Presumably, not so hard for the crime-solving professor!

A second example of this illusion comes from stand-up comedy. If you watch and listen to great comics, you marvel at their ability not only to tell very funny stories, but also the precise delivery of the punchline to those stories. With truly great comedians, I marvel at the symmetry of many comedic presentations when the comic starts with a theme at the beginning, moves through a series of stories, and then adeptly reintroduces the theme at the end. A sad manifestation of the "illusion of ease" and its dissolution is watching the uncomfortable presentation of someone at an open mic night who thinks they are funny because they somehow believe that their mundane lives can be transformed into something comedic or that it seems easy to do--you just stand up and talk about funny stuff. How hard can it be?

A contributing factor to this "illusion of ease" is how the presentation, lecture, or act appears seamless. The ideas flow logically, methodically, and entertainingly from one to the next. Transitions and segues are flawless, and the punchline, point, or conclusion is delivered with expert timing and precision. Often it is not understood by the audience that this seamlessness is the result of hours upon hours of preparation, and years of education, practice, and experience spent in becoming an expert. Therefore, what seems to look rather easy to others is an illusion. Ironically it is the years of hard work one has devoted to one's craft that creates this illusion!

The second theme, or misconception people have, is that many things can be attained with very little work. Depending on the field, a common idea is that it can take around 10,000-25,000 hours of training to become an expert at something. There is a reason why the trades define a master as someone who has first spent the necessary time as an apprentice, then journeyman before being conferred the highest standing of master. The same goes for academics, law, medicine, counseling, and many other professions. Also, in many professions, one deals with rejection. This is particularly evident in comedy, acting, and writing but also in other fields such as sales, and especially academics. I used to joke that "I could paper a wall with rejection letters." And it is true. Rejection occurs for many reasons. It could be due to a slowed job market, with too many candidates and too few positions. It could be due to other competing factors. It could even be because of one's inadequate preparation or training. But, when someone quips that they could do your job, remind yourself (and them) that it doesn't come easy.

* * *

Although They May Be Painful, They Are Not Dangerous

In May 1962 Stanley Milgram conducted his studies on obedience that went on to become one of the most controversial set of studies in psychology and the social sciences. In these studies, participants were assigned to be a teacher or a learner. However, the learner was part of the research team and the assignment to teacher or learner was rigged with the unwitting participant always assigned the role of teacher. The teacher was then instructed to deliver an electric shock when the learner who was placed in another room and hooked up to a shock generator failed to recall words from a set of word-pairs. The shock level started innocuously at 15 volts, and the teacher was to increase the shock level in increments of 15 volts to the maximum of 450 volts each time the learner recalled the wrong word. The purpose of the study was to see how far the teachers would go in providing electric shocks to the learner. Surprisingly, 63-65% of the teachers went all the way to 450 volts indicating complete obedience. Of course, anyone who has read Milgram's studies on obedience knows that wrong answers were deliberately provided and that the learner never received any electric shocks. It was all part of the ruse to make the teacher believe they were physically harming another person.

Milgram was part of a cohort of scientists that was interested in studying social change and the violent response by those in power to social change. For example, the studies on conformity by Solomon Ash and the Stanford Prison Study by Philip Zimbardo, along with Stanley Milgram's studies on obedience began to address why seemingly everyday people will engage in behaviors that they would otherwise not do.

For Milgram, not only was he influenced by the upheavals in the culture such as the civil rights movement, but also was intrigued by the rise of Nazi ideology and why so many people fell prey to its evil influence. Remember, his studies on obedience began only about 17 years after the end of WWII when the horrors of the holocaust were fully revealed. In the book, *The Banality of Evil*, author Hanna Arendt described how people who were relatively obscure, seemingly harmless, could engage in such horrific acts such as the holocaust. Although the book was mostly about Adolf Eichmann, who carried out the final solution, he was every bit the personification of evil but went about the destruction of millions simply as a problem to solve.

It could be argued that these studies on obedience were conducted over 60 years ago and would have little relevance today. For example, it is a litigious world we now live in, and it could be argued that first it would never be allowed, and second, no one today would go along with it or would reach the number of 63-65% complete obedience Milgram found in his studies. Milgram might disagree with that argument. Years later, in an interview with *60 Minutes*, he concluded that it would not be hard to set up a system of death camps in any town in the United States, like those found in Nazi Germany. And that it would be easy to find personnel to run the camps.

Every semester, I would show a 45-minute video of Milgram's studies, and it provided a very good heuristic to engage the students to do their own surveys of people on the street regarding obedience, but also to psychologically and behaviorally dissect why people obeyed even when they were perfectly free to leave at any time. However, after watching this video for what seemed like over one thousand times, I began to look more closely not at obedience, but at how the teachers were reacting toward and what they were saying to the experimenter. I noticed, of course, obvious signs of stress among the teachers, but I keyed in on what they said and how they behaved. Many would look toward the experimenter as if to get an assurance that although the learner was screaming in the other room to be let go and he was in pain, this did not seem to be enough for them to stop giving electric shocks. Others, seemed to indicate they were not responsible for what happens, others tried to seek clarification, where one teacher commented: "He kinda did some yelling in there."

Now of course, one of the signature responses by the experimenter to the teachers was: "Although they [the shocks] may be painful, they are not dangerous." After hearing this statement a thousand times, I began to think about our ability to really know the level of pain someone is in. Yes, the teachers believed the learner was experiencing pain and showed distress that they were inflicting pain on the learner, but I wonder if the context of the experiment with its level of credibility, and associated prestige of the University, along with the experimenter's clarification of pain caused enough confusion to interfere with the teacher's own assessment of the pain of another. For example, does "kinda doing some yelling" or even screams in of themselves indicate to us that someone is really in pain? And what awful implications that would have.

The treatment of prisoners of war has been defined by the Geneva Convention. However, after the horrific attack on the U.S. on 9/11, there was, justifiably, anger, outrage, and resolve to see justice done to the perpetrators of such a heinous crime. Although some of the perpetrators of the attack were dead, others with direct involvement and similar sympathies against the U. S. were incarcerated at Guantanamo Bay. The task then began one of extracting information to capture other criminals and to prevent future attacks.

To break the will of uncooperative detainees, the CIA with authorization from the President of the United States engaged in what became known as "enhanced interrogation techniques." These techniques included waterboarding, walling, forced stress positions, sleep deprivation, and temperature extremes to induce stress and discomfort. The Justice Department also defined "torture" in a narrow way. Inflicted pain could only be considered torture if it resulted in a serious physical injury such as organ failure or death.

Because of the nature of the crime, a new protocol of interrogation that possibly violates morality, ethics, and law could now be justified. But more importantly, with the introduction of terminology such as "enhanced interrogation," and the definition of torture, the United States government provided a permission structure that disturbingly echoes the experimenter in Milgram's studies: "Although they may be painful, they are not dangerous." It is also interesting to note that when we look internally at the levels of shock and percentage of people who disobeyed in Milgram's studies, we find that the highest percentage of disobedience occurred at the 150-v level, when the learner first expressed pain and was asked to be released. This may have been the place where the learner's rights became more important to the teacher than the necessity to continue the experiment. But also, it is the point in the experiment where the teacher was given clarity that the learner was truly experiencing pain.

The final disturbing implication of the misapplication of what we have learned from Milgram's studies is that it is in societies that embrace nationalism or authoritarianism that we begin to see an insensitivity to the pain of others. Although this blunting of our ability to be aware of the pain of others is caused by many complex factors, one that is clear is that we can reinterpret what it means to be in pain by manipulating our perception of it. The belief that harmful laws or practices are necessary for the greater good, or that our mistreatment of others although may be painful but not dangerous, or using semantics such as "enhanced interrogation," we mitigate our own guilt and culpability on the pain we inflict on others.

* * *

Seems Like 1984 Has Come Early

Talking with my younger self recently, I recalled the George Orwell novels *Animal Farm* and *Nineteen Eighty-Four*, and the predicted dystopian future that awaits societies that move toward a totalitarian system, where a ruling few oppressively govern and control all aspects of life. The result is loss of individual freedoms, constant surveillance, an inundation of propaganda, and manipulation to embrace "newspeak" and other authoritarian fictions of the state that are prescribed as "accurate" and "healthy" depictions of our social living and human experiences. It is a cultural experience where opposites become confused: Blind obedience to authority becomes the highest actualization of personal freedom; prejudice, hatred, and discrimination towards others is believed to express love and acceptance; a global society torn by conflicts becomes the autocratic realization of world peace. In my conversation with my younger self, who lived with the threat of mutual atomic destruction that arose during the Cold-War, I thought such an occurrence of that type of a society was just a haunting "science fiction." A social reality that might occur eons in the future, if ever. However, as my older self surmised, we do not always get it right at a younger age. And reflecting on the "state" of our current world, I offer that "it seems like 1984 has come early!" With this dystopian vision in mind, we take into consideration what we might do when we find music restricted or lose this form of individual and communal expression.

It is easy to become overwhelmed when bombarded with information 24-7, 365 days of the year. It is often suggested that we un-plug from this stream of constant information about the amusing exploits of celebrities, new social trends and fashions, exceptional human feats, and perhaps more often reported, political propaganda and the hurtful things folks do to one another. In the industrialized West, we have new terms such as toxic positivity, where despite the human suffering we might observe or personally experience, we purport that "everything will be okay," espousing a basic Pollyannish attitude that is taken to an unrealistic extreme. We have been conditioned to believe that we must always be "winning or doing better than our peers," and may have mistakenly come to believe that it is others who define and affirm our self-worth. Further compounding our feelings of disconnectedness is the fear of missing out (FOMO). This anxiety is exacerbated by social media feeds where we see people who have more "friends," more wealth, and more things than we could ever garner in our current living. Thus, we rue that we are not receiving all the best things in life, or that we feel we deserve. The regretful outcome is that our perceptions, feelings, and actions become the product of this distorted reality.

Music offers us a way to individually and communally reflect on our lives, and to overcome the perplexities and challenges that we encounter in our living. Music, in its sharing of symbolic meaning that may be transposed into one's own experience and emotional expression, offers a cathectic flexibility that nurtures adaptation and healing, and heralds a call to realize our deepest feelings of joy, hope, and love. Indeed, music offers an anthem that resounds in our self-expression of freedom, belonging, and contributions to causes that transcend the narrowness of our own self-interests. But what might happen if music was restricted or taken away from us? That we could not sing out or make sounds on our instruments to proclaim our willingness to take on life's challenges, to fight for a just cause, to hope to overcome those powers that would constrain ours or others' becoming? This may sound a bit macabre, but indeed there was a time during the medieval period (around 476 A.D. to about 1450 A.D.) when flatted notes were regarded as sinister and an expression of the Devil. Further, since the Scottish Jacobite uprising against the British government (1746 A.D.), native musical instruments like the bagpipe and others have been outlawed to extinguish rebellion and to suppress the cultural identity of those who would stand in opposition to the ruling authority. In the twentieth century, bans on styles of music such as jazz and rock-and-roll were enacted as these genres were regarded as immoral, idolatrous, or subversive. At our present moment, reasoning that music represents a form of moral corruption, the ruling Taliban in Afghanistan have placed restrictions on performing music and have gone so far as to destroy musical instruments, and to discriminate against and to threaten to punish people with floggings, fines, imprisonment, and execution if they violate this restriction. Yet, many Afghan musicians continue to create and play their music, often in secret performances and through various out of sight and underground exchanges. Moreover, as these young musicians report, the love of music and the expression of this art form is so vital to their identity that they will persevere regardless of the sanctions and threats they may endure.

Whether you see yourself as a musician or not, most of us recognize the exciting rhythms, soaring melodies, and lush harmonies of music that cast a captivating spell over the listener. Through its catharsis we find healing and revitalization of the spirit as we sing, play, and listen to our favorite songs and instrumental pieces. Where, as in the final movement of Beethoven's *Ninth Symphony*, we join in unison to announce an "Ode to Joy," celebrating hope and all the good things we discover in our living and relations with one another. Through music we may cast-off the dystopias that confront us and begin to create a world where empathy becomes the medium and currency we use and circulate to remind us of our great potential to self-actualize, to care for each other and to help one another along the way. In its anthems we find expression of our hopes to overcome life's greatest existential challenges, and to join in and contribute to the making of a society that embraces and celebrates personal freedom, equal rights, and justice for all.

As my younger self remarked, "you've really changed! These weren't ideas you expressed earlier in life! Gee, I think you might have learned something getting a little older!" And that is another point to make —like the different musical experiences we may encounter in our lives, we will all have unique and memorable experiences and in response become changed in an infinite number of ways. We live an experiential existence, always creating a new understanding of ourselves and the world we share with one another as we strive to become better people. We are always seeking an explanation and reason for our living. And like the conversation between my younger and older self, we can help each other by listening in a caring way, reflecting cooperatively, and holding onto each other as we find a way to move forward together. We can practice this experiential approach to our living by slowing down and stopping to observe and listen, actively reflecting on what we see and hear, and always endeavoring to see and hear the other person—as we would see and hear ourselves. It might mean playing a new piece of music or exploring other forms of musical expression—and if we try and take on these new creative endeavors, we may find we have changed, and like my younger self came to think—all for the better!

* * *

How Do We Define a Well Society?

How do we define a well society? Perhaps a more important question is *who* defines a well society? The answer to the latter question informs and directs the answer to the first. Who defines a well society is everyone. The importance of the person within the community, and the realization that the community and the person are one and the same, is the source of wellness. If we omit this individual-communal approach, then we are likely to have a society that only works for those with economic or political power. In a society such as that, and this is not uncommon in our current moment, the powerless have no voice. Those who are powerful, and thus more influential, in control and in-charge determine and define who receives basic resources and who goes without. When this occurs, people who live at or near the margins of society, those with the greatest needs and fewest of the essential resources, suffer the most. This disparity of wealth and resources is not an uncommon reality, but rather a common occurrence throughout the globe.

Further, if we look just within the U.S., a country with great wealth, we might assume we would see a rather equitable distribution of healthcare and life resources for all its citizens, but this assumption is far from the truth. Instead, we find an abject failure to care about, much less meet the needs of each person.

Unfortunately, the U.S. has a long history documenting the failure of our health care system. For example, in 1966, Martin Luther King, Jr. in a speech given at the *Convention of the Medical Committee on Human Rights* in Chicago, Illinois called attention to the inequality in health care as the most unjust as it shortens the lifespan of the person. This inequality in health continues to be fueled by hatred, racism, and xenophobia. It is grounded in the belief that certain individuals and groups are "unworthy" of the same rights that those deemed more "worthy" have. As we note at present, this judgment of unworthiness is driven by propaganda that suggest certain individuals and groups are somehow "gaming" the system and must be stopped, or that they are less than human and are rightly treated inhumanely. Again, it is the wealthy and powerful who determine worth in our society and this view is passed down to those who for whatever reason will believe it. The Covid-19 pandemic as well as current disparities in medical access reveal how the U.S. healthcare system is broken. Minorities were most affected by the pandemic. Higher deaths, and greater health problems occurred in these groups during the pandemic. As millions of people were getting Covid-19 and hundreds of thousands were dying, some health insurance companies reaped great profits even though medical appointments and surgeries were postponed during the pandemic. Yet, millions more have no healthcare due to preexisting poverty or loss of their jobs that resultantly caused loss of health insurance.

One might reason that if we adopt a communal perspective, we could apply the altruistic principle of offering and providing equal access to care for everyone as the primary and most crucial determinant of how to define a well society. The special concerns of moral philosophies such as consequentialism (e.g., maximizing the common good, minimizing suffering) and deontology (e.g., the duty to aid another person, free from the collateral benefits that one may receive) help to illuminate how we may determine a well society. Thus, a society that places the accumulation of corporate or personal wealth above the welfare of its citizens would be an unjust and unwell society.

When we finally recognize the personal autonomy, dignity, and human rights of each person, then we can begin to define what is a well society. A well society protects the personal freedoms, equality, and human rights of each person. A well society offers equal access to opportunities for its citizens to pursue personal life interests and forms of self-expression. A well society seeks an equitable distribution of resources, access to education, and pursuit of occupations. A well society seeks equitable access to exemplary healthcare, regardless of race, economic status, gender orientation, ethnic orientation, country of origin or immigration status. Indeed, a well society celebrates these moral ideals—it proclaims the need to hear every voice, to provide for each person's basic needs, and to offer the greatest promises that we might imagine in life.

The words of Dr. King and those who champion civil rights, the marches, and the songs we sing, such as "We Shall Overcome" and "Lift Every Voice and Sing," strengthen us in our struggle toward equality. As we seek to satisfy basic life needs, the existential concerns for survival, freedom, belonging, and self-identity, while perhaps always of critical personal concern, will always be requisite communal concerns.

* * *

Chapter 4 – Creativity

Whenever we create something, we also imaginatively fashion and create ourselves anew. As the humanistic psychologist Carl Rogers suggested, it is through our taking action and in our creating that we become transformed and move forward in realizing our greatest potential. Indeed, our creativity is the high-road to self-actualization and the attainment of our best self. Underscoring this humanistic orientation and the personal discovery afforded through our creative expression, in the essay, "Putting All the Pieces Together," Dean discusses how collage making can lead one to find personal balance and harmony. The ability to reorient or change perspective (i.e., "sideways looking") and its importance for our creativity and in finding meaning to one's life, is the subject of Scott's essay "Machine of Death..." Considering again how we might become involved in music, in the essay, "Playing Softly..." Dean highlights the importance of individual practice and ensemble playing that leads to deep personal satisfaction and connectedness to others. Miles Davis is provided as an example of how experimentation with different musical expressions, or "Coloring Outside the Lines" as Dean writes, result in musical innovations. Finally, to be truly free to create Dean instructs us to "Play, Have Fun! Do Not Be Afraid! Suspend Judgment!"

* * *

Putting All the Pieces Together

Each of us are more than the sum of all the parts that "describe" us. We are not definable by a single aspect of our reasoning, personality, relationships, occupations, or events from our past. We are more than all those features and representations–we are each an evolving, learning, and becoming person, always arranging and re-arranging the pieces of who we are as we seek balance and harmony in our lives.

A metaphor and practice for how we might go about living in a balanced and harmonious way is found in collage making. Collage making is the creative process of selecting and gluing various materials together to make art. Much like the philosophy expressed in the *Tao Te Ching*, the task in collage making is to recognize the many different elements that come together to make a whole–and to communicate in our creative work something that has not been expressed before. It is a task that seeks equilibrium and concord in our creative expression and living. Further, it is an approach that as we work with the uncertainty of how different pieces fit together, we become deeply immersed in our creative expression, finding release of emotions that provides illumination of other areas of our life and concerns for living.

As we consider how we might begin our collage making, we may opt for either a feature driven approach or a conceptually driven approach. The feature driven approach is one where we examine how particular aspects of one piece of the material that we are working with may come together and be arranged with other pieces to communicate a viable creative expression or idea. It is an approach that begins with no preconceived idea other than to see what happens. It relies on improvisation and a developing order that is imposed by the unconscious mind at first. Then, as the aesthetic expression arises and takes form, the conscious mind begins to exert its control to continue to shape and form the imaginative idea. Key features that define and provide us aesthetic pleasure are the object's beauty or artistic quality; the symmetry or balance that runs through it or forms the whole; the object's complexity or simplicity; the novelty or familiarity that is expressed; the object's proportional relations as well as its compositional and cohesive whole; the object's semantic content; its expressed symbolic meaning; and the physical properties such as shape, color, and texture. This feature driven approach allows the subliminal mind, the part of our mind that processes information with relatively little conscious constraint, to operate freely and direct the expressive arrangement of the various materials in our collage making.

Another method is the conceptually driven approach. This approach is much more directed by our conscious concerns. We may begin with the idea to communicate a specific meaning or express a particular emotion in our work. In doing so, the collage artist may make use of and choose almost any type of material, such as colored paper, rocks and pebbles, fabrics of different kinds, even fasteners like nuts and bolts. The collage then takes form as these materials are arranged in accordance with our preconceived idea. In a sense, this approach relies on a "conceptual blueprint," that directs our art making. For example, in the conceptually driven approach we might imagine a scene that we first sketch out, like a cactus abloom in a desert landscape, as shown in Figure 4.1 below.

Figure 4.1. D. VonDras, *Cactus Abloom in a Desert Landscape - Sketch*, 2024, pencil sketch; 4.25 X 5.5 inches.

From this sketch then, having our creative concept already in mind, we might work to find various materials that allow us to reconstruct the image. We might choose pieces of colored paper that we will cut from magazine photos that are then arranged and glued onto a substrate, as shown in Figure 4.2 below:

Figure 4.2. D. VonDras, *Cactus Abloom in a Desert Landscape - Collage,* 2024, mixed media; 4.25 X 5.5 inches.

In our art making, we combine our imagination with our technical proficiencies and conscious understanding of art principles. Thus, we begin with an idea of what we hope to communicate but are open to the uncertainty and novelty of how the features may come together, what might occur, and what might be expressed. Also, by allowing our subliminal mind to operate, we are free to experiment and discover a "new balance" as we construct and assemble the collage, or realize a "new meaning" that we find exciting and that communicates the creative idea or feeling in a novel way. This guided but relatively open to uncertainty approach is much like how we may experiment and operate in our everyday living. For example, we may plan on joining friends for lunch and catching-up on what is going on in their lives, but we may not know until we meet them and sit down together what we might select from the lunch menu, or what topics might arise in our discussion—we are open to the uncertainty and novelty of what might occur.

As we allow for uncertainty in our art making and in our everyday living, we become involved in an experiment of sorts. That is, we may have a set of possible outcomes in mind but are also open to see what might occur as we create and move forward in our experience. Again, everyday life is like this in several ways. For example, as we work with the uncertainty of our daily living, we may experiment to understand how best to satisfy our basic needs and find an inner balance and wholeness. Moreover, in our art making we tell a story about who we are and the way we see and operate in the world. Thus, as artists and as a people, we have the power and license to create and tell our story the way we choose. Knowing that as we live and think about who we are, we can at any time adjust our perceptions and worldview, change our context and media of expression, and revise our creative work and rewrite our story. Indeed, at midlife and in older age, we may discover new ways to arrange, re-arrange, and revise our creative work and the story of who we are and what we hope to become. So that, despite any constraints we may feel exist, concerns such as health limitations or not having all the technical abilities or resources, we may move forward in finding a positive balance in our life and fulfill our greatest potential.

As we take up our creative endeavors as part of our everyday living, we recognize the interdependencies we share with others. In our art and daily experience we communicate our questions and understandings about life, implicitly asking those around us for their opinion and involvement so that we may learn and understand more deeply the processes of art making and of living. For example, in one art making experiment one might consider working with homogenous elements (e.g., a shape, texture, or color) or introduce a novel characteristic, theme, or entity that requires the audience to reason and learn about. One interesting experiment is trying to create something that you have not tried before. In a sense asking, "Can I make that? Is that possible?" The experimental proposition leads us to ask, "let's see what might happen," and invites us into an orientation of being open about what might occur. One example is to make a collage using monochromatic pieces of paper, or as noted in the sketch and collages shown here, introduce an entity that may not be expected, and see what happens. An example of an experimentation using grey scale (a continuum of grey from black to white with no other colors) is shown in Figure 4.3.

Many of us, older and younger, because of our various social encounters may have reported after a particular interpersonal exchange that, "I felt like they thought I was from another planet, or that they were making fun of my clothes or the way I talked... that I was from outer-space – that I was an 'alien'." This idea of being the unfamiliar or unknown person is a phenomena that has drawn scientific interest as psychological researchers seek to understand the basis

Figure 4.3. D. VonDras, *Evening Farm,* 2024, mixed media, 4.25 X 5.5 inches.

for developing and holding xenophobic attitudes. Similarly, this notion of the unfamiliar, or the stranger, has become a focus of many artists' creative work. Introduced in Figure 4.4, and again, present in all the collages shown in this chapter is the image of a spaceship. There are perhaps many ways we might think about what the symbolism of a spaceship may mean; could it represent our own aging that we are not so comfortable with, or others we are not familiar with, or resolution and an acceptance of both these concerns?

Figure 4.4. D. VonDras, *Afternoon Visit*, 2024, mixed media, 4.25 X 5.5 inches.

Art's Multiple Meaning for Our Lives

Ladened with multiple meanings, the spaceship image in these pieces is intended to convey whimsy and playfulness. It is also intended to satirically portray that which we do not understand, or what is unfamiliar or unexpected, as well as something unknown that we need not fear. The spaceship or some other recurring surrealistic feature can also be used as a barometer by the artist to gauge how much the audience minds this aspect of the art. If at some point the art is considered and discussed in ways that looks beyond this unexpected or incongruous characteristic, then like the aims of the Expressionism movement, perhaps a particular human concern or existential realism that is expressed will be of greater interest to the audience. Resultantly, if the artwork contains aesthetic features deemed more important than the incongruous intrusion, then we might expect the discussion of the work to be much like the compliment given to the free verse poet after their prose reading, "We really enjoyed your poetry and its recitation–slang and all!"

But we do not have to be so judgmental as we look at and engage with artwork, listen to music, or watch a dramatic performance. When we are playful, having fun, free to express ourselves, and nonjudgmental in our art making and in our immersion in the arts, we may find there is a "spill-over effect," or a generalizability that flows into other areas of our life– that through our art making and creative involvements we also recognize changes in how we may look at the world, feel about ourselves and others, or think about what is possible and how we may move forward in our becoming.

Since early childhood we have all been artists, singers, dancers, drummers, and play actors. We have always enjoyed the fun and liberation of play–of entertaining ourselves as we are free to express and project our "true" self. By experimenting and "playing" in our collage making, we may also find new realizations about what our art expresses as well as the purpose and meaning of our lives

* * *

Machine of Death, Upside-Down Dalmatians, and the Creative Process

One of my hobbies is visiting second-hand bookstores. I visit these places with the excitement of an adventurer who hopes to discover a long-lost treasure. Often, I am rewarded by finding an out-of-print book (at a cheap price), or an interesting read, or a topic well off the beaten path. While kicking around one of these stores, I came across a book: *Machine of Death*. The title elicited from me several random death thoughts: "Death of a Salesman, Death of Marat, Mahler's Kindertotenlieder, Death Cab for Cutie, Megadeth."

Most people find a discussion of death a very impalpable topic and would rather stay away from a discussion of it all-together. It seems instead, that death is something that intrudes on us, either by experiencing the death of a loved one, or by a diagnosis of a terminal medical condition. Personally, I find the idea of death something that I cannot accept nor understand. To me death is a destructive event that snatches away beautiful people we love and leaves us with nothing in return. However, this is not an article about death but about the creative process.

Why I bought the book was because of the editors' intriguing question to the contributors. How would you write a story based on the supposition that from a blood sample, a machine of death could tell a person how they are going to die? The editors invited contributors to write stories about people who used the machine and were now confronted with a printout of how were going to die. The stories have quirky titles such as: "Flaming Marshmallows," "Vegetables," and, "Not Waving but Drowning." Not only are the printouts quirky but even something as straightforward as death by "Old Age" can be ironic. The editors point out that the prediction might mean to live to be very old or to be shot by an elderly person during a home invasion. The question, indeed, sparked highly creative writing from the contributors.

A common picture found in introductory psychology textbooks is the "spotted Dalmatian." The picture is comprised of black splotches that for most people looks like a Dalmatian eating out of a dog dish. It is an example of finding patterns in random data (pareidolia). When I presented this picture to students in my class, I would turn the picture upside down and ask them what they now see. Although it is an upside-down Dalmatian eating out of an upside-down dog dish, the replies would range from trees, to alligators, to faces. Like the book *Machine of Death*, this classroom demonstration allowed students to see something in a different, unique way resulting in innovative ideas and interpretations. I call this technique "Sideways Looking."

Although the term sideways looking is something I made up, the exercise itself is used in all media where one wants to invoke a new perspective to a topic and to jump-start the creative process. For example, the bassist Christian McBride hosts "The Lowdown: Conversations with Christian" on SiriusXM satellite radio, and "Jazz Night in America" on National Public Radio. In one segment of his interviews, he asks musicians to paint a musical "picture" on their instrument. He might ask them to "play walking in the snow at evening," or "play driving in a rough neighborhood." These questions allow the musician to create something on the spot.

A technique that jazz guitarist Pat Martino invented to produce creative ideas was to take a word or phrase and convert it into musical notes. How you do this is to write out all the letters of the alphabet:

ABCDEFGHIJKLMNOPQRSTUVWXYZ.

Then, underneath the alphabet write out the notes of a musical scale. It can be any scale, but here we will use the C major scale: CDEFGAB. Keep repeating the scale notes to the end of the alphabet. Those interested in ciphers and codes will notice that this is a simple substitution cipher:

ABCDEFGHIJKLMNOPQRSTUVWXYZ
CDEFGABCDEFGABCDEFGABCDEFG

You can now engage in the exercise to find your "musical name." So, for example we can now use anyone's name. Let's use Pat Martino and by finding the letters we can then find their corresponding musical note on the scale. The P becomes a D note, the A becomes a C note, and so on. When we find all the corresponding notes for the name Pat Martino, we see the note pattern: D C A A C F G D B C. This is thus the musical name for Pat Martino in the key of C major. Now one can further the creative process by changing notes, some to flats or sharps, varying the rhythms, converting the notes to chords, or moving to different keys. Again, this is an example of sideways looking. These two examples show to us that by a change in musical perspective, we overcome the mundane and hear new things.

We can also use sideways looking to see something in an unusual way (like the alligator in the upside-down Dalmatian). Here are two thought experiments. Look at the palm of your hands. If you were taking a class on creative writing and were asked to write about your hands, what would you write about? As you look at your hands, you could comment on how rough or smooth they were, or that each has four fingers and thumb. It would probably not get you high marks on the assignment. Now looking at it sideways, focus on the folds and wrinkles in your palms. What do they say to you? Perhaps you notice your lifeline and it inspires you to write about palmistry or the time you went to the circus and visited a fortune teller. Or you may see your fate line and inspire you to write about confronting and overcoming obstacles that you or others may have placed in front of you. You might write about what you did with your hands, your work, or the things you created with your hands. Another thought experiment is to look at a picture and try to see it in an unusual way. For example, look at a picture of a tree. I suggest a tree in winter with all its leaves gone. Now the picture itself could recall memories of winter days, thoughts of family, the times you looked at a tree in winter. But I also suggest turning the picture sideways or upside down and describing what you see or what it now suggests.

We probably do not need a machine of death or an upside-down Dalmatian to spark our creativity. However, a change in perspective is important not only for the creative process but also more broadly in how we find the courage to change ourselves. We can become weighed down by unfulfilling jobs, bad relationships, or other aspects of our lives that can lead to a sense of hopelessness and the belief that things will not change. Changing our lives requires the creative process. It is not easy to turn the picture upside down and see our lives in a new way, but even if we tilt it a little sideways, perhaps it is a beginning.

Playing Softly and "Tuning-In"

The changes we experience in our lives frequently evoke emotional responses. We often feel joy when we attain a transforming personal accomplishment like graduating from college, getting married, or being promoted in our job. We feel loss and sadness at the death of those we love. Similarly, our experience with nature and its daily cycle summons an emotional response from us. For example, we may feel a comfort in the calm and first light of early morning, or come to a point of rest in the encompassing quietude and relaxation of a sunset and the growing darkness of night.

Music also evokes emotions in us. We may feel overwhelmed by loud discordant electronic sounds that portray interpersonal conflict—perhaps sighing and remarking that, "that isn't music." Alternatively, we may find music to confer feelings of a peaceful respite from the cacophony of rush-hour traffic congestion and urban noise, such as in the soft and tender expressions of folk music and love songs, or in the delicate and clement sounds of a string ensemble.

Various scientific studies have shown that music entrains neurocognitive processes and innervates brain areas that produce neurochemicals associated with pleasant and comforting feelings (dopamine) as well as excitation and physical movement (adrenaline). As a result, in hearing musical sounds such as the soft whisper of the flute or the twangy sound of the guitar, our emotions, thoughts, and actions are stirred. It is not a big surprise then to find that many people enjoy and prefer to hear, sing, and play "love songs" that convey our deepest human feelings or prefer to listen to and sing-along with the hopeful expressions found in gospel or pop music. These styles of music connect with us at the deepest levels, and allow us to feel the enduring romance shared by lovers, the inspiration of overcoming life's challenges, or the longing for a world that comes together in unity, hope, and love.

In music we also find onomatopoeia-like expressions. An onomatopoeia is the formation of a word based on the sounds for which it is named. For example, we might think about the ways we reproduce the sounds of nature in the creation of words like "whoosh" or "kerplunk" to respectively portray a strong gust of wind, or a frog jumping into a pond. In media as varied as painting, poetry, music, and sculpture, we also find onomatopoeia-like representations that may communicate feelings as different and contrasting as desolation and coldness, or warmth and hope. In a like manner, we find expressive representations of the softness of a mother's caress and gentle love in Johannes Brahm's "Lullaby." In a similar way, we may recognize the representative excitement of our youth and coming of age in the rhythm and blues song "The Twist" by Hank Ballard, or the depiction of love and life's uncertainties in the ballet music of "Swan Lake" by Pyotr Ilyich Tchaikovsky.

"Tuning-In" and Enhancing Our Interpersonal Awareness

Through music too we also learn of ourselves, and may for the first time share in or find voice for many different sentiments and experiences of life. For example, we may share feelings of sadness and the heralding of hope after a tumultuous personal loss, as we may find in a song like "Tears in Heaven" by Eric Clapton and Wills Jennings, written about the death of

Clapton's four-year old son, Conor. At times too, the catharsis of music making and other musically expressive activities may allow us to purge and find release from past traumatic experiences, and a way to go forward in our journey. As we find in the MusiCorps Wounded Warrior Band rehabilitation program at Walter Reed National Military Medical Center, where soldiers wounded in combat learn or relearn to play music, and in the process find healing and a way to recover their lives.

As one learns and grows from their musical practice and ensemble playing, they may become more "tuned-in" and adept at understanding the interrelationships involving our perceptions, feelings, and actions. For example, it is often remarked by many older musicians, that while growing older presents new technical challenges (e.g., using alternative fingering patterns to accommodate rheumatoid arthritis, singing lower to accommodate loss of the higher range of one's voice), that they are "feeling" the music more than they ever have. Perhaps this reflects not only the many hours of practicing and performing, but also a lifetime of listening. Indeed, bearing in mind the many emotions and experiences music conveys, it should be noted that music listening may also help us "tune-in" and grow in our interpersonal awareness and development.

One method for "tuning-in" is learning to play softly when we practice. Indeed, for students of all ages and ability levels, playing one's instrument or singing is not just a matter of fingering, plucking, or precise enunciation of lyrics, it also includes the dynamic expression of musical sounds–the softness and loudness of the music that we create. Further, playing softly in our practice assists us in exploring and expanding our ability to execute passages that are intended to be softer or louder, but also in achieving a balance with other instruments and voices in the musical ensemble.

By gaining mastery in dynamic expression, we can delve more deeply into the feelings the music conveys. Whether pianissimo (very soft) or fortissimo (very loud), music entices and overcomes us–stirring us to action–allowing us to express feelings of gentleness, joy, hope, and excitement, or those of anger, drudge, and fright. For example, playing softly is important for trumpet players in their development of technical skills as well as melodic expression. Indeed, playing softly enhances both the achieving of correct breathing and wind support but also the right "buzzing" and pressure of the mouthpiece on the lips so that the musical notes can be flawlessly and sonorously sounded. These important technical aspects of trumpet playing also assist the brass player in acquiring the stamina to play longer musical passages, and to perform for longer periods of time.

Further, playing very softly, or playing with a "whisper" tone, allows the trumpeter to explore the very high range tones (the two octaves above the high C), with the correct lip buzzing and embouchure placement. Correspondingly, soft playing aids in finding and exploring the trumpet's pedal-tones (very lowest tones that range two octaves or more below the low F-sharp that is usually annotated for trumpet). When these very low and high tones are regularly practiced, one may develop greater tonal (timbre or color) and dynamic (piano and forte) expression of all the notes sounded, from the very low pedal-tones to the extremely high notes!

Practicing softly on other musical instruments is also recommended, as it similarly enhances dynamic expression and permits development of fingering and technical mastery. Thus in a compensatory way, when one can sing very softly, strike the piano key or drum head very softly, pluck the string of the guitar or draw the bow of the violin in a way that allows the string to vibrate very softly, then the somewhat soft (mezzo piano), somewhat loud (mezzo forte) and very loud (fortissimo) tone begins to sound richer, stronger, and more profound.

In our ensemble performance, playing softly and "tuning-in" allows other instruments in the musical conversation to be heard and an orchestral balance achieved. Similarly, applied to our interpersonal conversations, speaking softly is a way to show respect and encourage and engage in a supportive exchange of ideas, hopes, and dreams. Therefore, let us respectfully "tune-in" and listen to one another, paying attention to what each person has to say. In doing so we discover and appreciate what we have in common, and achieve a balance in our relationships.

* * *

Coloring Outside the Lines or
Just Miles Beyond

One of the great jazz musicians of all time is Miles Davis. With a career that spanned several decades, from the recording of the *Miles Davis Sextet* in 1945 to his final concert at the Hollywood Bowl in 1991, Miles played with many of the jazz legends and served as a mentor for many contemporary artists. It is a career that portrays both his creative and personal developmental journey.

Early in his career, as he was refining his art and building his reputation, Miles performed the classic jazz standards. Later in life, however, as he explored new styles of musical exposition and development, he broke with the conventions of the earlier jazz stylings to convey his own cultural and musical expressions. His later works show a willingness to continually experiment and discover where the musical expression may lead. Symbolically for the listener, in his later music there is the sound of freedom, of enlightenment, and always the sense that there is more to play and to say musically.

At age 47, Miles is noted to have remarked that his quest to continue to be creative and find artistic expression through his music led to new ways of conceiving what jazz might be. In this creative period, Miles' compositions were organically conceived and full of embedded cultural associations and inspiration. Miles' live recordings such as *Agharta* break with convention, emphasizing like an artist's palette, the desire to use improvisation and rhythmic and tonal experimentation to cast light on the deepest of human experiences. Indeed, the title of this live performance in Japan in 1975 has special meaning. In Sanskrit,

"Agharta" means the inner soul, a place of peace and tranquility, and in the music the listener may hear the artist's quest to go deeper into this inner space and place of being. To use the metaphor of the elementary school art teacher, some might say Miles was "coloring outside the lines."

Yet, Miles' subsequent creative works continued this experiment with jazz sounds and what is possible in terms of musical expression. We recognize the wide range of tonal color expressed in his music. The sounds can be dark and raspy, like the sounds of a saxophone, bright and pastel like the piercing and elan sounds of a muted trumpet, or earth-colored like the warm and supporting sound of the double-bass. Miles in his recording *Aura* features experimentation with a variety of tonal colors. Much like works by Arnold Schoenberg, Oliver Messiaen, and John Cage, Miles paints in a very abstract way, using tonal colors to portray emotional and intellectual experiences. Each with their own mood and feeling, the individual pieces are entitled "White," "Yellow," "Orange," "Red," "Green," "Blue," "Electric Red," "Indigo," and "Violet." Like many of Miles' compositions, these pieces reflect a quest for freedom, release of the artistic spirit, and hope and discovery of a new place and novel world of expression.

In many ways Miles Davis's music shows to us the many creative possibilities and contributions that may be made in the second half of the life course. Moreover, his creativity was not just portrayed in his music. In later life Miles delved into, explored, and used the lines, shapes, and colors of oil painting as another area of creative study and self-expression. Further, the imaginative and artistic insights offered through Miles' music seem to lift-up personal and cultural concerns, and place the creative expressions of jazz, a uniquely

African American art and cultural representation, as one of the greatest contributions to the world.

For us too, we may explore and look to "color outside the lines" or to go "Miles beyond" in our creative expressions. Whether we are making or listening to music, painting, drawing, dancing, acting, writing, knitting, sewing, or exploring our creativity in other ways, we too can find and realize a deeper awareness and understanding of our living, and in our inventiveness express new insights into our life's purpose and meaning.

* * *

Play! Have Fun! Do Not Be Afraid! Suspend Judgment!

Singing and dancing, drawing, making art, and play-acting are creative activities that most of us enjoyed as children. You might have been in a seasonal concert or special Holiday play, exhibited your work in a high school art show, or performed a recitation of a poem for an assignment in middle-school. In many ways, we have been immersed in a variety of imaginative activities since early childhood. Moreover, our creativity has offered us opportunities to explore different styles and ways of self-expression. Yet, as we have grown-up and taken on new responsibilities, we may have left behind our earlier artistic interests. Perhaps because we felt it was not an essential activity for us as adults, or we could not afford living as an "artist," or felt our singing or music making or other creative endeavors were not good enough. Despite these reasons, however, involvement in and self-expression through the arts is beneficial for our wellbeing. In singing, dancing, music listening and music making, drawing, painting, carving, and knitting, we find new inspiration, discover new ways of seeing the world, and gain insight into the next steps in life we might take or paths we may follow. In sharing what we create, we connect with others and are revitalized by their support as we move forward in becoming who we were meant to be. But if we have stopped being creative, or find it hard to become involved again with the arts, how do we rediscover the creative processes we enjoyed as children?

A first step is to realize that there is no age limit to when we can be creative. As Connie Goldman has suggested, our creativity is an expression of the human spirit, and whenever we take up our artist's "tools" we begin again to express the essence of our spirit. Further, as Marianist Brother A. Brian Zampier suggests, working on something every day, even just for 5-10 minutes, can help us discover the joy of our creativity again. Always active in sketch booking, Brian offers the following guidance to help us reconnect to being creative:

1) Play!

2) Have fun!

3) Do not be afraid!

4) Suspend judgment!

Following these four simple rules provide us the freedom to develop and learn new techniques that enhance our creativity. According to Brian, making art is fun when we approach it as a playful activity. As play, we can just have fun doing it. And, it is the fun part that makes us want to learn and do it more. When we engage in play, we are free to create. We are unafraid of whether what we made is "good enough" as judged by ourselves or others. What we create when we play is determined by our own sense of imagination and self-realization.

Following this approach, I have developed and pursued a daily regime of making music and sketch booking. In the process, one of the new forms of art explored is collage making, using recycled pieces of paper from magazines and junk mail. Along with pencil sketches, the collages are of various scenes I have observed or imagined. Each image is intended to tell a story. They reflect times when we enjoy being with others, marvel at the beauty of nature, partake in an exciting adventure, feel an inner calm, or find inspiration in the moment. Like the drawing of children playing in a splash-pad in Figure 4.5, the sketch art is intended to be whimsical and express joyfulness.

Figure 4.5. D. VonDras, *Having Fun at the Splash Pad,* 2024, pencil sketch, 4.25 X 5.5 inches.

The collage shown in Figure 4.6 depicts the peace and calm of a beautiful mountain lake in early July! A daily practice of music or art making offers the opportunity for personal reflection and contemplation, as well as brief respite from the mundane and other concerns of our daily living. A time, as artist Janice Mason Steeves suggests, where we may contemplatively enter into a sacred space, rediscover ourselves, find healing, and reflect upon and commune with nature.

Figure 4.6. D. VonDras, *A Lake Adventure,* 2024, mixed media, 4.25 X 5.5 inches.

In the collage shown in Figure 4.7, the calm and quiet of a meditative garden is communicated.

It should be noted that the same guiding principles about being creative shared by Brother Brian also apply to singing, making music, and other creative activities too. For example, one summer I took up the challenge of composing a daily musical exercise to enhance the practice of a young trombone student. The musical exercises were simple and brief. And, what quickly became clear was that this "musical sketch booking" was a way to make the practice session fun! The short compositions can be of any musical style and tailored to the preferences and ability level of the student. Further, the many "miniature" pieces that are created can later be combined to represent a larger musical work.

Figure 4.7. D. VonDras, *A Tranquil Place,* 2024, mixed media, 4.25 X 5.5 inches.

Again, we can use the principles of playing, having fun, being fearlessness and non-judgmental in other areas of our creativity. For example, you might embrace these simple rules as you learn to sing or play a new piece of music you especially enjoy. Similarly, like Scott, who along with his guitar playing and town band involvements has also developed a practice of daily poetry writing, we might create and keep a book of poetry and prose writings, or a personal journal of our self-reflections and new life discoveries, and in the process delve more deeply into knowing ourselves and contemplating our life experiences.

We are never too old to be creative and to share what we invent or make with others. Ultimately to engage in the creative process means to also let go of those things that hold us back. Thus, play and create fearlessly, do not be afraid of what sounds may come from your clarinet or trombone, or whether your poetry, sketching or painting is "good enough" to share with others–suspend seeing and evaluating what you create as being "good" or "bad." Embrace an attitude of experimentation, looking to see what happens and what is possible. Our creativity tells the story of who we are–it is a narrative expression of our aspirations, yearnings, resilience, and triumphs. We may not always be satisfied with our latest creative expression, but we all can improve when we continue to practice what we love to do.

* * *

Chapter 5 – Things that Go Bump in the Night

Ghost stories and the odd and eerie feelings that we all have experienced are the subjects of this chapter. Tales of ghosts and spirits, like religious and spiritual allegories, tell us of our deeper psychology for sure. Suggestive of transcendental beliefs and possible other, supernatural worlds, ghost stories are found within all cultures and reflect our universal quest to resolve the existential concerns of being and non-being, freedom, belonging, and identity. Thus, ghost stories, while often being scary, also convey and provide us a hope of a life beyond our current existence, and a way we may stay connected or happily united with past relations and modes of reality. The first essay, "A Personal Ghost Story (of sorts)" by Scott tells of odd staircases, birds in the attic and a screaming macaw. Considering a phenomena akin to ghost notes (i.e., those places in a musical score where the notation indicates a rhythmic value but no pitch is indicated and thus no tone sounded), in the essay "Cats, Ghosts, and Other Creatures..." Dean first discusses the important connection among humans, animals, and music, and later tells a humorous story of "spectral and ghost like sounds" that late at night are heard emanating from a haunted guitar. Emphasizing manifestations of the supernatural, the classic campfire story is told in Scott's "A Terrifying Ghost Story." The chapter ends with Scott's reflections on cozy mysteries in, "It's a Mystery!"

* * *

A Personal Ghost Story (of sorts)

New to the area, my wife and I were invited to the home of a colleague for a welcome dinner. The house was pre-civil war era. As we walked through the door that led us directly into the spacious living room, I noticed the room was divided by two tall pillars. Directly across from me was a large stone fireplace and beside it was a full-size carnival merry-go-round horse–the one with the wild eyes, flared nostrils and bared teeth. In the room were two live macaws that were the pets of the owner. She told us that they were very chatty and that one of them occasionally made a sound that sounded very close to a woman's scream. She told us this to prepare us not to be shocked when the bird belted one out. Well, as soon as she warned us, the bird let out a blood-curdling scream!

The dinner was very pleasant. After dinner, our host invited us to a tour of the house as she said it contained some very interesting features. The house had three stories with a fourth comprising the attic. Over the years many additions and rooms had been added to the house. These additions gave the house a ramshackle feel as if it was something from a Dickensian novel. One prominent feature our host pointed out was that the staircase leading up to the second story contained an extra step. As we walked up, I noticed that the angle of the staircase sloped less than a regular staircase and that as you reached the top you felt that you indeed took one step too many.

We surveyed the 2nd floor rooms. As we went into one of the rooms with windows that overlooked the street, our guest abruptly turned to us and said, "I have to tell you that previous occupants and guests have reported they have seen a ghost in this room." She went on to tell that the reported ghost was that of a woman seen weeping over the crib of a crying baby. I want to add that the town and surrounding area is rich in the history of ghosts of the civil war, and the story goes that this woman–the ghost–was reported to be wearing clothes from that period. Of course, at that point we heard the macaw from the living room let out a deathly scream! My nerves were beginning to be shaken. Although I do not believe in ghosts, the story itself, the oddness of the rooms, and the histrionic macaw were beginning to affect me.

Then, our host mentioned to us that she rescued birds. Thinking, that seems like a very honorable thing to do, she then asked us, "Do you want to see them?" I did not know what to think or say, so I stupidly said, ok. She led us to the 4th floor, which was the attic, and opened the door. Here inside were what seemed to be 50-60 birds, some flying around, others perched anywhere there was a place to land. She said that she finds them, rescues them, and brings them to stay in the attic. To me the behavior of these birds reminded me of that Hitchcock movie as some of them I believed were staring at me from their perch ready to peck at me unmercifully. At that point my nerves had had enough of old houses, weird staircases, ghost stories, and birds in the attic.

As we were heading back down near the top of the oddly built stairs, the macaw let out an ear-piercing scream! I yelled out something not repeated here and in one leap jumped the remaining stairs and flung open the front door. I stopped myself and went back inside. Here, I found my wife and our friend sitting on the bottom step laughing themselves silly.

As a post-script to this story, our friend asked my niece if she would stay in the house and feed her birds while she was away on vacation. My niece agreed and the friend showed her how to feed the macaws and the rescued birds in the attic. I have to say although it seemed weird and possibly unsanitary to have these birds confined in the attic, she did provide a regular feeding schedule with nutritious food and instructions on how much and what type of food the birds should receive. While staying there one night, my niece called my wife and asked if there were any cats in the house as she said she heard what sounded like a cat or maybe a baby crying. My wife, reminded of the ghost story and other people's encounters, and not to frighten her, told my niece that it was probably a cat outside. Later when the friend came home, my niece mentioned the experience to her. A dark, solemn look came over her, and she said to my niece not to worry about it, it was probably nothing. When our niece mentioned what our friend said, we felt obligated to tell her about the ghost of the weeping woman and the crying baby. Needless to say, in the future when our friend asked her to feed the birds, she would only do so during the day and never again stayed overnight!

* * *

Cats, Ghosts, and Other Creatures Bumping in the Night

In our book, *Celebrating the Arts of Living: Pathways to Joy and Fulfillment in Later Life*, we noted the comfort our pets provide us, and presented a special section about Dr. Milton H. Dunsky who played recordings of classical and jazz music for his pet dachshunds while away at work, and how his hounds provided love, comfort, and support to him during the last days of his life. Not to leave out felines and other animals from our discussion, in this essay we also acknowledge other interactions between humans and animals involving music. Indeed, not only does the animal-human relationship reflect our need for pets and the unconditional love that pets provide us, but it also highlights the importance music plays in our lives and in the life of animals. Our relationship with animals is expressed in songs like "Cat Scratch Fever," "Eye of the Tiger," "Hound Dog," in albums such as King Crimson's "Lark's Tongue in Aspic," Al Stewarts, "Year of the Cat," and in bands such as "The Stray Cats," "Snarky Puppy," "The Eagles," and "The Animals."

When we make comparative analyses between humans and animals and their involvement with sound, we find fascinating similarities and differences. For example, dogs are recognized for their ability to hear very high pitches, detecting sounds well beyond the range of humans (67 to 45,000 Hz, versus 50 to 20,000 Hz, respectively). However, while the family dog is well known for its acute aural sensitivity, the family cat has an even greater range of hearing than dogs (45 to 64,000 Hz), and in comparison to other creatures we note that the hearing of the mouse (1000 to 94,000 Hz), the bat (2,000 to 110,000 Hz), the beluga whale (1,000 to 123,000 Hz) and the porpoise (75 to 150,000 Hz) are even more sensitive to high-pitched sounds.

We also observe the very interesting, almost human-like, ways animals respond to music. For example, on several occasions late at night, during piano rehearsal of classical music pieces, a cat has arrived outside my window eerily singing along as if they were harmonizing or offering a "call-and-response" to the music. This phenomenon is explained via a reaction to the often purring-like sounds of classical music that are preferred by the feline. It should be recognized, however, that cats are not alone in their preferences or response to music, suggesting that music somehow communicates aspects relevant to social-bonding and of social-being for both humans and other animals as well.

Dogs and cats do not always get along, but like cats, dogs also enjoy the soothing properties of classical music. However, dogs show rapid habituation (i.e., a decrease in responsiveness to the musical stimuli after exposure) to symphonic music and thus lose interest quickly and easily move on to other activities that capture their attention. Yet, being very different from cats, who best like music composed for "cats," (i.e., music that mimics the rhythmic and tonal qualities of a purr or meow), dogs also show a preference for and enjoy the reggae and soft rock human-styles of music. These music genres may have even deeper and more sustained calming effects for dogs, as noted by enhanced heart rate variability indicative of decreased stress, and the dog spending more time lying down than standing when these styles of music are played.

Extending the human-animal-music interaction further, I have observed house wrens perched on the sill outside my window, or nearby on the porch gutter, looking into the practice room while I play musical scales and arpeggios on the trumpet early in the morning. It is always nice to have a perceptive audience, and a sense that one's music is appreciated. And, certainly, house wrens may be thought of in that way. Indeed, regarded as musically sophisticated, house wrens are recognized as great virtuosi of bird song, with some males singing up to 194 different types of songs. Which of course are of great interest and closely attended to by the female of the species. With a vast song repertoire, the house wren's songs are noted to contain falling and undulating sounds, much like the sounds of major and minor scales and arpeggios played throughout the full range on the trumpet. Their songs are full of rhythmic chirps and chips, as well as melodic trills and whistles.

While we have noted bird songs, it should also be recognized that many animals sing. And more than the bull-frogs croak, the dog's bark, or a cow's moo, there are many types of songs sung. Including the Mexican free-tailed bat's mating ballad, the humpbacked whale's self-identifying crooning, the gibbon's social bonding duet, and the gorilla's joyful hymn sung while eating. Thus, through the sounds of music and song, humans and animals communicate about and celebrate their life experiences. Indeed, even the house mouse has a repertoire of songs used for expressive communication between males and females, and with mouse pups, singing in the ultrasonic range of 22,500 to 50,000 Hz.

Furthermore, humans who are keen to the notion of social communication between species, like Dr. Milton H. Dunsky and his dachshunds, also endeavor to interact with and involve other animals in their appreciation of music and celebration of life. Thus, we note that there have been piano concerts played for monkeys, musical performances provided for dolphins and whales, and even very entertaining demonstrations of synchronized dance movements set to music that feature a "grooving" cockatoo.

The human-animal-music involvement, however, does not just draw our attention to the natural world, but also to supernatural phenomena. In this area we note various cultural assertions that connect humans and animals to music-like expressions of the paranormal and mystical, such as the notion that the "cock-a-doodle-doo" of the rooster can signal danger, symbolize good fortune, or predict a catastrophe of biblical proportions. But the catching of a ghost and the exploits of a little mouse are worth mentioning too, and that is described in the following "ghost story."

The Ghost Guitarist

The house was haunted, so the story goes. As evidence of a haunting, the homeowner reported hearing strange sounds late at night, coming from a seldom played guitar that sat in the corner of the living room. These resonances, according to the homeowner, were quite erratic and unnerving. Sometimes the guitar sounds were played on the low-sounding strings, sometimes on the high-pitched strings, and sometimes all the strings at once. Further, these ghostly musical expressions were usually abrupt and often dramatically loud. The homeowner, determined to get to the bottom of this strange phenomena and not wishing to be driven out of the home, stayed up one night to confront "the ghost." Sitting in the dark for an interminable amount of time, she again heard eerie sounds coming from the guitar. Immediately switching on the lights, with amazement she saw a little mouse jump out of the guitar's sound hole. It was later realized that the mouse had made a nest in the guitar, and at night when leaving and returning had to press through the strings thus creating these spectral and ghost-like sounds. We do not know what happened next involving the homeowner and the mouse, or what high pitched expressive sounds the mouse may have made when surprised by the light. However, the moral of the story may be to practice your musical instruments, so that furry friends do not take up residence in them! And if you do have ghosts, insist that they pay rent!

* * *

A Terrifying Ghost Story

The campers were sitting around the campfire enjoying the warm glow after a day of fishing and hiking. One of the campers asked another, older camper to tell them a ghost story. He was the oldest of the group, probably in his early to mid-seventies. A somber expression came over him and in the traditional campfire-ghost-story fashion, he placed a flashlight under his chin and turned it on. The glow of the flashlight along with the light from the fire gave his face an unnatural expression of sunken cheeks and dark hollows for eyes. He began:

> It was fifty years ago that I moved into a house because the rent was cheap. I later came to realize that the house was truly haunted. As I did not believe in ghosts, I often joked that if there were ghosts where I lived that they would need to share in paying the rent. However, I found that this little joke was little comfort in the harsh reality of this supernatural experience.
>
> It started when I first drove up to the place. The house was the kind that had the garage directly under it and not adjacent. I pulled my car in front of the garage door. The door was one with a row of glass windows along the top of it. As I was waiting for the landlord to show up, I thought I saw a face looking out one of the garage windows. The face was that of a man with dark hair and dark beard. Thinking that the landlord was already

there I got out of my car, and as I did the landlord pulled up beside me in his car. It should be noted that the landlord although having dark hair was clean shaven. He showed me around the place, and we settled on the rent, and I signed the agreement. I somewhat forgot about the earlier experience of the face in the window but can say I was still unsettled by it.

The storyteller stopped and said, "Hey, someone throw another log on the fire before it goes out." He then continued his story:

From day one, I never felt comfortable there. I always felt as if someone or something was watching me. These feelings of being watched at times became so strong that I had to leave the house and go outside for them to subside. One incident occurred when I was sitting on the couch watching a football game on TV. The door to the cellar was in the living room and while watching the game, I was overcome with a sense that something was behind the cellar door. If any of you have had this experience, you know how hard it is to overcome a gripping fear and do the rational thing of simply opening the door that would dispel any fear and apprehension. However, the fear of being watched became so oppressive that I could only jump off the couch and run out the door!

By this point in the story, the group of campers were so engrossed in the tale that the fire was left to a few embers and was in danger of going out altogether. The old man kicked around the embers with a stick and continued:

I had this feeling of being watched many times and often could not sleep through the night and be awakened by what felt like a huge pressure on me, or at times felt like someone was throwing a heavy blanket over me. I would immediately wake up in a sweat. I also saw the face several times when I was in the yard, it was looking out of the kitchen window. One time I was mowing the yard. The backyard went up the hill from the back of the house and the property was adjacent to a row of trees beyond which ran open property up the mountain. I was at the far end of the back lot of the property and looking down at the house, I saw the face in the window again looking at me! I decided that I had had enough. Fortunately, I was near the end of my rent agreement and informed the landlord that I would not renew it. When he asked why, I told him about my experiences with the feeling of being watched and the face in the window. A dark expression came over him and he said, 'I see, it makes sense.' He told me that the previous renter was a professional magician. In the garage he had built a labyrinth of rooms made of plywood and two-by fours that the landlord later surmised were not intended for magical entertainment but something more sinister and likely satanic. The landlord related that he and the magician had a falling out over the rent and the magician left in anger and placed a curse on the house. Once I left and moved to a different place, the feeling of being watched left me and I slept peacefully and could sit on my own couch without dread. I tried over the years to come to an understanding of my experience. Perhaps because the house was situated by an unpaved side road that ran up the mountain and that to the side of it about 100 yards from the house ran high tension power lines. Perhaps, that was the source of my uneasiness, as I had read that high tension electrical powerlines or powerful EMPs might create in a person sensitive to these energies, feeling of dread and even reports that something was watching them. Perhaps it was this along with the fact that I was going through a very stressful time in my life and that somehow, I was letting my imagination run away with me. However, I never could resolve this experience, and having had it only when I lived in that house, and never since then, I can only conclude that the house was truly haunted.

Noticing that the fire had completely gone out, he ended his story, switched off the flashlight, and everything went dark.

* * *

It's A Mystery!

My wife enjoys reading mystery novels. Although she has been stumped a few times, she typically guesses who the murderer is before the end of the book. I personally do not read mystery novels. However, we both enjoy watching mysteries on television together and subscribe to several channels that deliver hundreds of shows from which to choose.

We prefer watching what are called the "cozy" mysteries. These are the ones that have quirky, interesting characters, and although the murders may be gruesome, they are not portrayed in any graphic detail. We shy away from the dark, brooding characters, who bring too many personal problems to the story. We find these as highly distracting. Or the shows that describe the murder in every gory detail, or where the story line is dark (such as involving missing children, or serial killers). In "cozy" mysteries the characters may have a dark, hidden past, and are very serious when it comes to solving the murder, they still bring the ability to inject humor into the storyline. At some point we started noticing several themes that seem to be used in most of the programs we watch. Together we came up with a list of common themes and common main characters in these mysteries. These lists are not based on any formal tally or frequency analysis, but more on our intuition and gut reactions. You may have your own list. But if we are watching a story, and we both say "Yep, that's the _____ theme" then it makes its way onto the list.

Common Themes (not in any particular order):

- Death in the Vineyard

- The Haunted House

- The Christmas Mystery

- The Rock (country, rap, reggae, etc.) Star Murder

- Ones Involving Caravans or Travelers (usually found in the British mysteries)

- The Family Curse

- Death of an Athlete

- The bachelor or bachelorette party murder

- The murder at the Fair (or circus, or any other fete)

- The land (or company) takeover by big corporation or developer

- Those involving restaurant kitchens, bakeries, etc.

- Dance clubs, Cricket, Football clubs, etc.

Common Occupation of the Main Character with Examples:

- The Chef or Caterer: "Pie in the Sky," "Mrs. Sidhu Investigates"

- The Professor: "Harry Wild"

- The Disgraced Detective: "Jack Taylor"

- The Rule-Bending Detective: "A Touch of Frost"

- The Retired Cops: "New Tricks"

- The Clergy: "Father Dowling Mysteries," "Sister Boniface," "Father Brown"

- The Writer: "Murder She Wrote," "Castle"

- The character who recently lost or divorced a spouse or partner: "My Life is Murder," "The Madame Blanc Mysteries"

We do admit that most of these themes and characters come from the "British" mysteries as we find the "American" versions either too violent, or too one-dimensional. Those typically involve gratuitous shootouts, explosions, and characters who seem to be spending more time cleaning up their personal affairs and too little time solving the case. This is not to say that these do not occur in the "British" versions, but we tend not to watch those either. We find it quite humorous in the shows we watch that the "British" detectives who are typically unarmed approach the knife-wielding or gun-toting criminal with the goal of "talking" them into giving themselves up. And with the flourish of "You've been Nicked!" The criminal politely says, "Ok, you got me, Gov." Now that I think of it, I will say though that the "Hallmark" mysteries also fall under our category of "Cozy" too with its cavalcade of bakers, chocolatiers, and librarian sleuths.

We can also think about why we like to watch a good mystery and what makes it one that is watchable. Adapted from the 10 essential elements of a mystery story website, good mysteries contain the following characteristics: (1) A strong hook. The first scene should compel the viewer to continue watching the program; (2) Setting. Here the key is location, location, location. Exotic places, quaint villages, historic settings (such as "Foyle's War"), for example, are pleasers; (3) Crime. Obviously, but the crime too should pique the viewer's interest. A shooting is not very interesting, but a body found in a wine vat, provides a different flavor (pardon the pun) to the mystery; (Numbers 4 and 5) Sleuth and Villain. Obviously. But again, the characters are interesting, possibly quirky, and maybe put the viewer in a "love-them-hate-them" relationship with the characters. I add that a supporting cast of interesting characters, such as the pathologist, subordinates, colleagues, sidekick, or senior officer enhance the interest and entertainment value of the program; (6) Momentum. The story must move along. It should not get bogged down by a lot of side stories, or flashbacks that leave the reader to figure out their relevance. And importantly, it should not take more than one or two episodes to solve the crime and bring the criminal to justice; (7) Clues. Seems obvious. But again, the viewer should be presented with clues that help them piece the story together, but also contain red-herrings, or false clues, sprinkled in to keep the viewer guessing as to who might be the culprit; This is also number (8), the Red Herring; (9) Foreshadowing. The story increasingly becomes more sinister, dangerous, with a sense of foreboding and is barreling toward a climax. For example, the sleuth may be exploring a dark warehouse without being aware that the villain is lurking in the shadows; (10) A Satisfying Ending. The story resolves, the criminal is caught, loose ends are tied up and clues make sense. Also, we like happy endings where the sleuth and adjutant characters are sharing a drink, a meal, and where one of the characters ends the show with a humorous quip.

To end this piece, I came up with ideas for characters, along with possible titles for the series, that would violate most of the 10 elements of a good mystery:

- The Crime Solving Uber Driver: "A 5-star Review of Murder"

- The Model Airplane Builder: "Flying with the Dead"

- The Insurance Adjuster: "Insurance can be Murder"

- Package Delivery Person: "Dead on Your Doorstep"

- Automotive Mechanic: "You can't Repair Murder"

I did not say these were going to be great ideas! Keep watching!

* * *

Chapter 6 – Getting Older and Interpersonal

More that 2000 years ago, the Roman statesman Marcus Tullius Cicero in his essay "De Senectute (On Old Age)" wrote of various-physical declines and a kind of public humiliation that is often experienced in older age, but also suggested the astuteness and ripening of intellectual insights that may be expressed in later life. Indeed, older age is more than a time of physical or mental decline and social ignominy. It is also a time of new opportunities for creative expression, of personal renaissance, and perhaps a time when one will make their greatest contributions to family and community. Using community theater as a backdrop, Dean in his flash fiction piece, "Cast as a Non-Speaking Character," emphasizes the feeling of neglect, isolation, and irrelevance when one is perceived to be "old," but also the special insights and gifts that older adults have to share with younger people. Scott continues how older folks are viewed negatively in the essay "How to be Ageist," and ways to dispel false beliefs about older age. Similarly, Dean offers hope as he describes five ways to wellbeing and the art of taking care of one another in the essay, "What We Can Accomplish with a Little Help from Our Friends." The counterintuitive essay, "If it is Hard, Don't Play It," by Scott challenges us to reach our goals but with less effort.

* * *

Cast as a Non-Speaking Character:
A Short Story

It is mid-afternoon in late spring. The story's protagonist, a retired older man, is reclined on a couch in a comfortable living room, surrounded by many books and family memorabilia. The story begins with the protagonist's reflective observations:

Though peeking through silvery-grey clouds from time to time, the sun had slowly moved behind the big tree in the front yard, and I was just starting on the daily crossword puzzle when my cellphone rang.

The caller-identification indicated it was from the Community Theater. I thought, well this might be the call about my audition for the role of the Stage Manager in *Our Town*, Thornton Wilder's play that was being planned for production later in the summer.

Suggested to be one of the greatest plays ever written, but certainly attracting criticism for its singular portrayal of white culture, implied puritanism, and nostalgic lament, Wilder's play explores the cycle-of-life and the various existential challenges we meet as we grow up and take on new responsibilities, enter into romantic relationships and leave home, come to understand the brevity of life, and uneasily confront personal loss and the death of those we dearly love.

I always loved that play–and the Stage Manager's wise and all-knowing narration. That would be a great role for me! I thought.

As the phone continued to ring, I answered, "Hello!"

The voice on the other end said, "Mister... uhm... uhm..."

"That's me!" I replied.

The caller continued, "Oh, hi! I'm Sheryl, and I am calling to let you know that we, the Theater Audition Committee, really appreciated your audition for the part in the play *Our Town*... but we had several excellent actors try out... and you were not chosen."

She stopped for a moment, then continued. "However, we, the Committee, thought you would be great for another part," she offered.

"This would be a non-speaking role–someone to be part of the town group that gathers at the back of the stage in Act 3, the cemetery scene," she said.

"We, the Audition Committee, think you would be great in that role!" she emphatically stated.

There was long pause. I thought to myself, am I being "punked?" Is this for real?

In a rather uncomfortable way, I asked, "A non-speaking part?"

"Yes, that's right... you would play one of the town's people in the final act," Sheryl said.

"A non-speaking part?" I asked again.

"Yes," she said.

"Okay, you really had me going there 'Sheryl!' You are just calling me to 'rattle my chain' a bit aren't you?" I comically suggested.

"No," she said. "Just to let you know that you didn't get the part... but that we, the Audition Committee, think you would be great as a town person in Act 3," she further delineated.

There was another long pause. Feeling disappointed, I thought to myself, after all these years, and I am being selected for a non-speaking part. I seem to have enough problems just getting older and feeling that society doesn't care about us "senior citizens," that maybe my life has no purpose anymore. But being cast in a non-speaking role–almost a non-person role–well if that doesn't take the cake!

Feeling a rising level of personal indignation and continuing my self-reflective complaint, I thought that when a person gets older they deserve the respect and consideration that is offered to everyone–at any age– young and old. It seems to me that everyone should be treated with respect and recognized as a vital part of the human family. Even if there may be an ebbing of intellectual prowess or physical ability, a person can still make a significant contribution in life–to their family and community. Even if it is only to help others understand the challenges of growing up and growing older, or the tragedy and difficulty when illness is encountered, or when an illness chronically endures. Worse yet, when dementia occurs. Being asked to take a "non-speaking part" feels like I have been asked to sail off into oblivion–that I am headed for a great divide, traveling alone to meet death.

After the long silence I said, "Oh, I am sorry then... I was just hoping to get the part." I continued, "You know... that's a great play! I didn't realize it when I was younger... but I think my grandparents and parents were teaching me something about later life... about what it's like getting older... and what we might still do."

"They seemed to express an insight that was not communicated easily... or that I did not understand when I was younger... or maybe I was just focused on my involvement with the 'younger generation'," I said.

"I realize older people need younger people–just like younger people need older people... to fully express ourselves... to feel a part of the human family... and older people... we have so much to still share and give to everyone... our wisdom... our insight about ways to cope with life's challenges, and about death... even if our enlightened teaching may be overshadowed by illness or waning capabilities... there is still a lot to learn from us 'older people'... and many things that we may share with younger people... maybe it's our love for life and joy for living... or one's courage to continue despite the various hardships experienced as they grow older... encountering illness but still holding out hope... even when death comes closer..." I said, trailing off.

"I remember the stories my grandparents used to tell me!" I exclaimed. "It was important to hear those stories... it seems their real meaning is only being revealed to me now... now that I am older," I encouragingly stated. "I know this may be sounding a bit like a *senior's soliloquy* perhaps... but there is a great deal to learn from us older people!" I avowed.

"There are many things to work out in life... especially as we get older... we have to face our own mortality... and resolve the anxiety that continues to surround the complexities of our own lives and the ending that we seem to be racing towards that lurks on the horizon... and whatever may come after that..." I said, trailing off again.

There was another long pause, and with new strength of voice I said, "You know, in our care and concern for each other... younger and older people... families next door and down the street and on the other side of town... heck, even families on the other side of the world... there is something to be said about the greatness and yet simplicity of our humble existence... about the sacredness of each person's life... and the great gift of each person... even the person we might not get along with very well or care very much about..."

Again, resetting my tone, I continued, "We all play a special role in this grand drama... we invent, reinvent, and manage the many different and important concerns of our life... we share in creating a reason and purpose for our lives... even when we get very old... and perhaps then, as my grandparents and parents seemed to express and tell me... showing me in how they lived... and sometimes it was just with a look, a smile, a wink, a nod... without words... without speaking... that especially in older age, we have lots to share and many gifts to give to one another... perhaps the greatest gift is just telling about our lives... our ways of looking at the world and hopes for the future... and expressions of our love... and that at any age, 'life' is still worth celebrating!"

There was a long pause again. I looked outside and the clouds had continued to gather, now in steel-grey and dark purples hues, and had overtaken the skyscape.

"Sheryl? Still there?" I asked, apologetically.

"Yes... still here," she said.

"I've got my calendar out now," I said.

With curiosity, I asked, "So when do rehearsals start?"

* * *

How to be Ageist

In psychology we talk about three "ISMS:" Racism, Sexism, and Ageism. Racism is the "inability or refusal to recognize the rights, needs, and dignity, or value of people of particular races or geographical origins." Sexism too denies the rights of a person based on sex, or gender identification.

Definition of Ageism

Ageism is when we let the age of the person influence our perceptions of that person. Ageism–and the other "isms"--is based on our stereotypes (how we think), prejudice (how we feel) and results in discrimination (how we act) toward others. These stereotypes, prejudices, and discriminatory practices can be directed toward both younger and older people. It affects our judgments of the person's ability, perceived attractiveness, and competence, to name a few. A simple example is that although the person has the requisite skills, training, and ability, we may believe a person is not competent to do a job specifically because they are perceived to be too young. Or, that a person may not be capable of continuing in a job specifically because they are perceived to be too old. We will focus more on ageism as it affects older adults although we recognize that ageism is prevalent throughout all stages of life.

How to be Ageist

We are all ageist to some extent. The insidious feature of ageism is that it is implicit. That is, we may engage in ageism and not be aware we are doing so. We learn implicitly and explicitly our stereotypes, prejudices, and discriminatory behavior largely through our culture. As a result, we devalue the older person's abilities, character, and intelligence, and any perceived deficits in these features are judged as "typical" of the older person. Ageism is inculcated into our worldview and becomes manifest below the level that we are aware we are engaging in it. We will outline three ways that ageism can occur by using an example, let's call him Jerry. Jerry has been with the organization for many years, and although older and is past the age when he could retire, he feels he can still do his job. But there are some folks in the company who want to force Jerry into retirement because they think he is too old, although he continues to have the highest performance record in the history of the company. Now let's look at the 3 ways those in the company reinforce their ageist beliefs and myths regarding Jerry and his age:

False Belief 1: We believe that Memory Defines Intelligence

Jerry at times forgets a person's name, he can no longer speak extemporaneously and must bring notes or use a PowerPoint when in meetings, or falters when asked a question.

False Belief 1 Dispelled

The relationship between memory and intelligence is quite complicated. As we get older, we can maintain what is called crystallized intelligence, that is our memory for things we have learned, and the wisdom, and skills we have acquired can be with us possibly throughout our lives. This is why musicians well into their later years can still play music from memory because they have well-practiced it and it has become implicit. However, we do see changes in fluid intelligence; we tend to slow down or have more difficulty when it comes to learning new tasks or to respond quickly to a question or to think quickly "on the fly." However, those folks who continue to maintain interest in acquiring new knowledge and are naturally curious tend to perform much better on memory tasks than those who do not.

False Belief 2: We Confuse Speed with Ability

Jerry is no longer as fast as he once was. He takes time to answer a question. As he ponders his answer, his gaze may look to others as a vacant stare. He no longer joins in the company's physical activities at their annual picnic.

False Belief 2 Dispelled

Unfortunately, ageism affects our perception even of simple behaviors. A gaze from an older person who pauses to ponder their answer to a question may be perceived by some as a vacant stare, but the same gaze may be interpreted quite differently when it is attributed to a younger person. We may slow down in some areas. We may not be quite as agile as we once were, but we also learn to compensate for any apparent slowing. Again, this ability to adjust, and often we adjust quite well, to age-related changes shows a rather remarkable sense of practical intelligence.

False Belief 3: We Confabulate Disability and Age

Jerry has had a stutter since childhood. He has learned ways to control his stutter, but at times he stutters especially when under stress, tired, or is required to respond to a question quickly. As he has become older, his stutter has become more pronounced and noticeable particularly at meetings when he is speaking.

False Belief 3 Dispelled

History unfortunately is clear that people have negative views of those with disabilities. Folks with disabilities are perceived to be less capable, even less intelligent than their "able" counterparts. Work, housing, and education discrimination are well-documented in our society toward people with disabilities. These negative views and discriminatory practices become more pronounced when one looks at the age of the person. The Americans with Disabilities Act (ADA, 1990) was designed to protect people with disabilities from discrimination regardless of age.

But again, why would we do this? Why are we ageist when we see memory lapses, reduced speed, agility, and disability in an older person? Why do we immediately jump to the judgment that they are no longer capable of doing a job or worse, that they can no longer be a contributing, functioning member of society? Maybe these questions occur because we experience an existential threat to ourselves when we look at another. Recognizing that life is difficult (a first principle in Buddhist thought), we also wish to propose that ageism—and all "isms"—spring from four existential concerns: existence, freedom, social connection, and personal identity. The faltering of an older person poses to us an existential threat on all four counts. In response to this threat, we inappropriately blame that person. In psychology we call this the fundamental attribution error. When we commit this error, we attribute the person's behavior to something about them personally–in this case their apparent "cognitive and behavioral decline" to their age, but fail to appreciate how outside, external factors, such as lack of sleep, virus, or cold, and other stressors may be contributors to their functional acuity at that moment. The most insidious reaction when we commit this attribution error is to aggress against that person in the form of various social exclusions (e.g., ignoring the person, direct sabotage of that person's goals, biased characterizations) and physical actions that range from the simple interpersonal slights to the potentially lethal disregard for the older person. Perhaps witnessing another's struggles triggers the uncertainty of our own future and abilities. Rather than reacting with empathy and offering support, we may feel that they are a threat to our personal freedom, confidence, and initiative. Specifically, our sense of personal invulnerability is shattered with the realization that one day we will be that age too. That is frightening! So, one way to relieve our anxiety is to diminish or devalue the older person in some manner. It is a hard lesson to learn that maybe it is the uncertainty of our own existence and not the age of the person, that is the real root of all "evil."

As a final thought, we propose two possible endings to our story:

Ending 1

Jerry was forced to take an early retirement. A year later the company went into receivership.

Ending 2

Jerry became CEO of the company. That year the company reported its highest quarterly earnings in the history of the company.

* * *

What We Can Accomplish with a Little Help from Our Friends

We often fail to acknowledge the tremendous amount of aid and assistance from family, friends, and others we meet as we travel on our life's journey. Early on, those who cared for us as children played very special roles in our lives as we grew up and became adults. They helped us as we entered school and prepared for jobs and careers. Other folks as well provided direction and advice along the way. Teachers, coaches, bosses, friends, and co-workers shared their insights on how to be successful in life, and provided moral support as we met challenges in our living. As adolescents and young adults, many of us may remember a special person who helped us to move forward in a positive way. At midlife and in older age, we have also discovered new friends who offered their assistance when we faced the challenges of illness, job downsizing, retirement, or loss of family members or close friends. As we reflect on how others have come to our aid, we realize that we too have an obligation to take care of those who need help.

But each person has their own way of expressing this obligation and caring, and in turn, feeling that they are loved and cared about by others. So it is no surprise that these personal idiosyncrasies are difficult to identify and hard to satisfy at times. For example, in a study that asked about the relationship between perceptions of social support and the tangible symbols of caring one may receive while in the hospital, one participant who received many get-well cards and bouquets as he recovered from an illness, remarked, "Yeah, they'll send cards and flowers, but they won't mow the yard!" Clearly, despite the well-wishes and out-pouring of concern by family members and friends, this gentleman did not feel overly "cared about." In contrast, an older person who received no cards or flowers while they were ill, noted the bolstering comfort of her spiritual beliefs, while the only material expression of care and concern came from an occasional telephone-call from her daughter. Thus, we understand there are many variations in how we might give and receive and express our care to one another. Further, we also appreciate that each of us may need and require the assistance of others as we recover from illness or injury, reconsider next-steps in our jobs or as we prepare to retire, face unexpected economic or family situations, make transition to different housing arrangements, or need extra help in our everyday living. These concerns often bring with them a need to self-evaluate and make adjustments in how we are living.

Indeed, as we move through life, periodically we will self-evaluate what is important for us to do and what we hope to yet become. In this self-evaluation process, we are likely to sense a need to make life-style adjustments as we revise our identity or re-define our sense of purpose and life meaning. Certainly, in later life we have moved beyond the concerns of childhood and young adulthood—times in development when we might have worried about completing our schooling, finding work, forming an intimate relationship, and living on our own the first time. At midlife and in older age, how we measure success in life may become less based on the milestones we reached or awards we received, but rather on how much we have given to others. This generative orientation to take care of others, children as well as younger and older adults, is a central concern for us in midlife and later adulthood. In a related way, this caring orientation is also a key instruction found within the cultural traditions of people throughout the world. Indeed, three communal values shared across cultures include offering charity and aid to others–especially children, those who are ill, the elderly, and those who are less fortunate than us; being modest and expressing a humility that regards and treats others as equals; and, telling the truth and being honest.

As a curious and communal species, we seek an explanation and try to understand our lives. As noted by the renowned scholar Huston Smith, many of the world's religious traditions offer us a set of rules or principles that provide a framework for living and how to be in the world. These guiding instructions, whether conveyed in the Judeo-Christian model of the Ten Commandments, the Hindu Seven Stages of Enlightenment, the Five Pillars of Islam, the Eight-Fold Path of Buddhism, the philosophy of the *Tao Te Ching*, or the Oral Traditions of Indigenous Communities, suggest ways of moving beyond the most self-centered and base concerns we may hold, to an orientation of respecting and caring for one another and the earth. In Hinduism, this transcendence may be described as moving from "getting" to "giving," where we shift from seeking personal gratifications and obtaining things (e.g., material objects, awards, social status), concerns we have in childhood and early adulthood, to an orientation beyond these ego concerns, where we may freely give to others and selflessly serve in our communities. Correspondingly, as many humanistic models of development characterize, from times of our youth to late in life, this type of self-transcendence and personal growth is important to our living authentically, with positive purpose and meaning. Moreover, this sensitivity to and awareness of our interconnectedness compels a re-orientation of how we live that gives meaning to our lives and enhances our sense of personal wellbeing.

You, Me, and Five Ways to Wellbeing

As we consider caring for one another as an aspect of our personal growth, it is interesting to note how the give-and-take of our social involvements is keenly represented in each of the "Five Ways to Wellbeing" outlined by Susan Hogan and Emily Bradfield from the University of Derby in the United Kingdom. As these researchers suggest, the five major drivers of wellbeing are connecting; being active; taking notice; keep learning; and giving. Further, Hogan and Bradfield suggest these drivers are often found within a variety of creative pursuits we may undertake. For example, our community involvement and support relationships serve as a buffer against mental ill health at any age, and "connecting" relationships that are encouraging, supportive and meaningful often come about through one's participation in a community choral group or orchestra, traditional folk-dance club, sewing group, as well as other hobby or artistic activities where one may meet with others who hold the same creative interests.

The complement of "connecting," is "being active." Like supportive social exchanges, being active is suggested to enhance wellbeing and lower rates of depression and anxiety. In a similar manner then, attending a concert, going to a community theater performance, visiting a quilting show, or other community and civic events where one may participate and be with others is recognized as a driver of wellbeing.

Again, we are a curious and communal species, and thus processes of self-reflection and mindfulness are key aspects of the third feature that moves us toward wellness, "taking notice." As Hogan and Bradfield suggest, reflections upon our creative activities and processes may bring about artistic excitement and satisfaction, that along with other cathartic effects, also enhances our coping and general wellness. Thus, how we may understand and appreciate our audience's response to our art, dance, music, sewing, singing, or other creative work, is another form of "taking notice" and engaging in a social way.

Learning, as recognized in the theories of Lev Vygotsky and Albert Bandura, is fundamentally a social experience. We learn from one another as we work together, share ideas and perspectives, and discern new ways to adapt and move forward in a positive way. Thus, we again find social processes involved in the fourth characteristic that moves us toward wellness, "keep learning." When we do things like add a new piece of music to our performance repertoire, experiment with unconventional subjects or unique perspectives in our drawings, introduce a novel color palette in our painting or quilting, try different patterns in our knitting, we offer ourselves new intellectual challenges as well as stimulation that serves as a counterweight to cognitive decline.

The fifth and final wellness driver, "giving," underscores the interpersonal exchange that has occurred throughout our lives. As noted by Hogan and Bradfield, the social behaviors of helping, sharing, and caregiving have been found to be correlated with enhanced self-worth and positive feelings. Thus, in many areas we may beneficially give of our talents, of our creativity, of our time, of our wealth, and not only enhance our wellbeing, but also the wellbeing of those who are benefactors of our giving. As retired social worker Angela Glendenning suggests, the limits of our "giving" are only restricted by our imagination. So, let us expand our sharing of compassion, encouragement, and practical support, and go beyond what is expected in our caring and service to one another.

The Art of Taking Care of One Another

From time to time, we all need a little help from our friends. An interesting phenomenon seen in many drive-through coffee shop and fast-food restaurant queues is the "pay it forward" practice. It alludes to the "treat others as you hope they may treat you" way of operating in the world. We can "pay it forward" in many other ways too. Whether it is a wave or a smile to a passerby, practical assistance to a neighbor, or just letting someone know we care about them by sending a note or card. In doing so, we may move forward in our transition from "getting" to "giving." There is an art to taking care of one another. When we seek to understand the other person's needs, in a sense "walk in their shoes," we often grow in our insight and compassion towards them. Moreover, as we look to see others the way we see ourselves, we may encounter, as philosopher Martin Buber suggests, a dialogical transcendence where we experience the highest form of reality or aspects of the Divine. Thus, in the process of growing as a person, we may further refine our art of taking care of one another through our compassionate listening, expression of unconditional regard, and kind responding. Indeed, when we convey our warmth, recognition, and friendliness, or offer our encouragement and assistance, we practice the art of taking care of one another, and leave a legacy of empathy, compassion, care, hope, and love. And what greater artistic accomplishment could there be?

* * *

If It Is Hard, Don't Play It

The legendary guitarist Joe Pass once said: "If it's hard, don't play it." We add: "If it's not fun, don't do it." At first read, the advice of don't play it if it's too hard, don't do it if it's not fun, seems to say that one should not work too hard or to go beyond one's comfort zone, but these statements imply the opposite. This article, then, is not about playing it safe. It is about challenging yourself and reaching beyond what you thought was possible. It is also about not wasting your time and effort on that which has no value.

But to reach beyond and to challenge yourself in ways that lead to success, we must first look at what holds us back from achieving our goals. Why do things become hard, or are no longer fun? We can do the things that are hard, as well as those that are easy and fun, but we must first look at two false assumptions.

False Assumption 1

We make the false assumption that for life to have meaning it must be hard and we must struggle. The response to this is that often the difficulty we encounter is because we make things too complicated. The key is to simplify. One way to simplify is to look for alternative approaches that result in success but by an easier route. Joe Pass's statement was intended to show guitar players a better way to approach playing. Rather than trying to manage complicated chord voicings, he recommended simplifying your approach by creating 3 note chord voicings. He also proposed that all chords are made up of the dominant, minor, and major. This recommendation can be applied to how we live our lives. If your life is too complicated find out why. A lot of people work hard, but for some reason their work does not prosper. Is it that their expectations go beyond what the work would yield? Are they working ineffectively? Joe Pass instructed that when we play guitar it should convey motion, freedom, and play what you hear and feel. Perhaps life should be that way too? We move gracefully, with freedom, and guided by our inner sense of what we truly want, feel, and who we are.

False Assumption 2

We must keep trying even when we know we will never succeed. The response to this assumption is to break away and discard those things that hold you back. Is it an abusive or dysfunctional relationship? Is it over-dependence on others? Is it the fear of failure if you try something new? Although there is something apparently noble in an existential way of continuing the fight when all hope is lost, we must soberly assess whether the cause is worthy of the struggle.

In life and in playing the guitar, we must keep learning, build a reservoir of ideas, find new, constructive relationships, keep our existing relationship healthy, train, practice, and re-evaluate what is important to us and what achieves our goals in a positive way. There is a Zen philosophy that states: "Take the time to enjoy your work." Thus, our "work" that we call life is to be approached as something joyful.

Finding Your Sweet Spot

I have come to believe that the key to optimum playing is finding the instrument's sweet spot. Every instrument has one. It is the place where it has the best tone, where you can articulate very well, and moves you to play at your best. We also understand the concept of sweet spot in other areas. In sports like golf, baseball, or tennis there is a place on the golf club, bat, or racket that one can identify as the sweet spot. In an instrument such as the guitar one can find the right set of strings, the right set up, and intonation that allows the instrument to play at its best. With an electric guitar, the interplay of the amplifier setup and the guitar work together to find that spot. This applies to other instruments as well. With proper set, say of pads, reeds, mouthpiece, we can find that sweet spot.

It is not just the proper set up of the instrument that creates the sweet spot, but also the interaction of the player along with the context in which the instrument is played. The musician must come to the performance with the right mindset, the right attitude, and the right approach to their instrument. The venue must have proper acoustics. Support from the venue staff and the audience is important. The same goes for athletes. Not only does one need the right bat suitable for that person's grip and stance, but also the person must have a connection with the equipment that they are using. For the musician, this connection can be explained as a sense of oneness, something spiritual, and transcendent. Also involved is experience. Through practice and training, one comes to understand the instrument and where the sweet spot is.

The Sweet Spot in Life

Playing music is a metaphor for how we find the sweet spot in our lives. Keep in mind that this is not easy and many of us struggle with things that not only keep us occupied with cares and concerns, and looming dangers, which makes finding a sweet spot almost impossible. We all have felt like we are getting nowhere or that it always seems like it is one step forward and two or more steps back. But the key is that we must continue to find a way where we live our lives most fully. Not only in music but in life we can do the following to find our sweet spot:

Stay engaged. Keep practicing, keep playing. Get up and do things. Have hobbies, play with your kids, go out on date nights, listen to concerts. Do anything that interests you. By being engaged you connect to others.

Be curious. Always take the time to learn new things. Marvel at the world around you and the people in it. If you play an instrument, try playing new scales, unfamiliar tunes, and different and odd meters.

Look for opportunities. Try something new. Go to open mic nights. Play in jam sessions. If asked to fill in for someone, do it. You make your own success by seizing upon opportunity.

Keep learning. Read everything you can about any topic. Always learn more about your instrument and reflect on the insight others convey about their experiences. Understand history, not only the history of society, and culture, but also your own personal history.

Don't get too loud. Interestingly, this suggestion applies to our own personal interaction with others and to how we play our instrument. We are uncomfortable around people who present themselves in a boastful, boorish, and loud way. Always listen first before speaking or interacting with others. The same goes with playing your instrument. Although the common joke is to turn everything to 11, just as sitting at the front of the banquet table and being asked to move because the seat was reserved for someone else, as the biblical text tells us, it is always better to play soft and then be asked to turn it up. Being asked, or more likely shouted at to turn it down, creates unnecessary tension and discontent. One interesting technique is to play as softly and as quietly as one can when practicing. For horns and other wind instruments, this practice, although challenging at first, will contribute to greater stamina and control of one's playing. For the guitar, particularly electric guitar, turn the volume on the guitar and amp to a point where the acoustic (un-amplified) sound of the guitar is balanced with the amplified sound. That is, you can hear both. Working and adjusting your instrument this way will allow you to attain that sweet spot. Not only will your instrument be at its best, but you will too. And isn't that what it's all about?

* * *

Chapter 7 – The Everyday Skeptic

We are all "common-sense psychologists," motivated to explain our thoughts and behaviors, and the thoughts and behaviors of others. These explanations are often not based on formulated scientific evidence, but on our own intuitions and guesses. In many ways this type of psychology is a practical way to understand the world, but it can also result in biases and errors in judgment. In this chapter Scott looks at how everyday, common-sense psychology is used to understand what are often biases and errors in our perception and judgment. The poem "I Saw Truth" presents the fragile relationship that exists between truth and freedom. Offering a satirical take on soothe sayers and prognosticators, Scott considers how anyone can be a psychic in the essay, "I Only Consult Guaranteed, Authentic, Certified Psychics." With tacit reference to one's sense of personal control in one's quest to find happiness, and the implicit biases these existential concerns may produce, Scott explains the power of the infamous "Blue Dot" to bring us fame and fortune in "The Blue Dot is Back!" Why we take risks or fail to take them and how they affect our feelings of regret or satisfaction is addressed in "The Counterfactuals of Counterfactual Thinking." The chapter concludes with Scott's poem "Not Uncommon Experience." Although we may feel that others' lives are more interesting than ours, the poem shows that maybe the experiences of others are not much different from our own.

* * *

I Saw Truth

I saw Truth the other day.

He wasn't quite what I imagined
him to be.

He was walking down the street,
Clothed in the light of the new-
born day.

As anthems played from his shirt
pocket,
He smiled.
He was brighter than the brightest
light.

Flinging his spoken wisdom to the
far corners of the street,
Hoping to be heard.

He was walking with his friend,
Freedom.

While talking they chewed up the
stupidity of humankind,
And spat out the waste made
clean.

From their eyes fell droplets of
light,
Making bright the darkened skies.

I was walking in the distance,
Flying with my own thoughts as
    my
Boots clattered with the sidewalk.

I passed them, blinded by some
    electric storms of my own.
And dodging the garbage that was
    flung at me...

I shut my eyes.

I saw truth the other day.

He wasn't quite what I imagined
    him to be.

He was lying in the street,
Spat upon and trampled into the
    dust,
Until he could hardly be seen.

There were eight billion mourners
    at the funeral,
But no one cried.

Freedom asked for a ride home,
So, I put her in my shirt pocket,
And walked on.

* * *

I Only Consult Guaranteed, Authentic, Certified Psychics

I only consult guaranteed, authentic, certified psychics. Just a look at the websites makes it obvious they are your best choice to handle all your paranormal needs. With their guidance, you can understand your life path, make decisions about love, career, and health with the goal of finding true happiness. Of course, one should avoid those psychics who do not carry the prestige and validity of being guaranteed, authentic, and certified. At the rate of the low introductory price of $1.00 or less per minute up to $4.99 per minute after 5 or 10 minutes, psychics who do not have the trifecta of being guaranteed, authentic, and certified, are just "taking your money." And of course, always look for positive reviews and testimonials from "satisfied" clients.

Although research has demonstrated that even when a claim of paranormal ability is debunked, many people will continue to believe that there may still be something to this. Of course, some of the explanations are that the failed prediction was due to a bad reading, unclear forces, or even the insincerity of the client. It is somewhat paradoxical that warning an audience beforehand that a psychic reading was a simple magician's trick increased their belief in the paranormal. It is also interesting that informing the audience afterward decreased their belief in the paranormal, somewhat. However, I think this paradox can be resolved by looking at how people handle conflicting information. I would propose that people engage in a type of cognitive dissonance where now both psychic and non-psychic explanations need to be resolved. One outcome of this reaction to conflicting information is what I call the "yeh, but..." response.

This "yeh but" occurs when people are given a plausible, normal, and even more scientific explanation of the paranormal claim, and they discount it by offering a single example to support the claim--the "yeh, but." It is like the person who is informed that smoking causes cancer replies with, "Yeh, but my grandfather smoked a pack of cigarettes a day and lived to be 95!" Even a mountain of evidence debunking a false belief is leveled by this simple phrase. We thus give more validity and pay more attention to a claim that supports our belief than to one that discounts it.

The intriguing question is why do people continue to believe in psychics? One is that people have a need to explain the unexplainable. The experience of Déjà Vu, or even a profound experience of having seen a ghost, an eerie feeling of being watched, or having a premonition must be resolved. To us, then the only way to come to terms with these feelings is to attribute them to some paranormal force. These are extraordinary experiences that require extraordinary explanations. The psychic can provide these extraordinary interpretations.

Another explanation is that people believe there is so much evidence of the paranormal. History is replete with soothsayers, mystics, and psychics. Famous examples include the Oracle of Delphi (Pythia), Cassandra of Greek mythology, clairvoyant, Edgar Cayce, and many others. TV shows such as The Unexplained, and Paranormal Investigators add to the sense that the paranormal is all around us. In the area where I live there are at least twenty paranormal investigators, societies, and ghost tours. It is not to discount that many people do report unexplained feelings and experiences. When events in our world disturb and upset us, we need to find an explanation for them. This search for an explanation though can make us vulnerable to misinformation.

Adding to the perception that the paranormal is everywhere and in all facets of life is the common misperception that psychics are routinely utilized in police work. Websites abound of psychics claiming that they have worked with police forces and have helped solve many crimes. Popular crime shows and books add to this inflated perception of the psychic's involvement with the police. It is interesting and implausible to believe that in over 150 years of forensic science the police become so "stymied" by a crime that their only hope is to contact a psychic. The question of whether a psychic is successful in solving a crime, or whether police departments routinely use psychics in their police work, is answered with a resounding NO! A much-cited study conducted by Sweat and Durm, in 1993 interviewed 50 (48 responded) police departments in the largest cities in the United States, found that 65% (31) never used a psychic and those that did (35%, or 17) reported that the psychic was not useful. These numbers are confirmed with a more recent survey of 102 law enforcement personnel conducted in 2012, who were asked if they personally used a psychic in their investigation. Here, 28.4% indicated yes and 71.6% indicated no. However, scientific data is no shield against the psychic who simply claims they are used by police departments and have solved many crimes.

James Randi, magician, and psychic debunker who died in 2020 would offer a 1-million-dollar prize to any psychic who could demonstrate a paranormal feat that Randi could not replicate using illusion or magic. No one was ever able to claim the prize money. The million-dollar prize challenge ended in 2015 not because a psychic was successful, but because the foundation decided it would better serve the public by converting to a grant making foundation. Undaunted, however, it is easier and more effective for the psychic to simply tell others they are good, guaranteed, authentic, and certified rather than be challenged by damning evidence to the contrary.

I leave with my personal experience of why evidence often fails to debunk a belief in psychics. When I talked about ESP in class, I used a demonstration where a psychic guessed a card chosen by a student. The trick involved having a student pick a card out of a deck of cards and then call a psychic on the phone who would then guess the card selected. The way this trick works involves a confederate (in this case my wife) who poses as a psychic and a system to code the cards. For example, each card was matched to a different "psychic's" name whom the student was then to call and ask for. For example, if the selected card were a jack of diamonds, I would surreptitiously look at the code sheet and tell the student to ask for Madame Zaranda. If a different card were selected it would be coded with a different name, such as Madame Opal for the ace of spades. My wife would have the code sheet in front of her when the student called. She could then compare the name to the corresponding card. When the student called, my wife would go into a routine such as for the jack of diamonds, "I see the figure of a man... He is elaborately dressed...," and so on. Then she would guess the card to the astonishment of the class. It is surprisingly a very vivid and entertaining demonstration. The point of this article though is to highlight the tenacity of a false claim even when the trick is revealed. After I explained the ruse and showed them the coding sheet with corresponding names, I had several students come to me after class and asked for the number of the "psychic" as they would like to use her services! In this case, the psychic (my wife) did not need to be guaranteed, authentic, or even certified. It was then that I realized I had chosen the wrong profession!

*　*　*

The Blue Dot is Back! And so are Illusory Correlations!

It's been around since the 1990s. Originally published in the *National Enquirer* tabloid, this image of a blue dot when rubbed will endow the person with untold wealth, good fortune, and health. Since its first printing, the blue dot has been published many times since then and various websites now invite you to download their own version of the blue dot. The lucky blue dot story is filled with testimonials by people who have won lotteries, won new trucks and cars, and had their failing health restored. The reason the blue dot works presumably, is that it is infused with a psychic's good energy and if one rubs the blue dot this positive energy will be transferred to you, and you will be on your way to fame and fortune. It should be noted that over the years, the psychic had to reinfuse the dot with good energy, I guess because the good energy battery eventually runs down or something like that. Even casinos are on board and welcome players to bring their lucky blue dots with them. It sure beats having to worry about card counting!

Before you plunk down your money on the latest issue containing the lucky blue dot or download it from a website, we might consider first why people believe the blue dot might work and why it most likely does not. Let's consider two explanations: Illusory correlations and the power of a testimonial.

Illusory Correlations

It is quite common to connect events together. For example, we can reasonably make the connection that studying hard results in a good grade on a test. Or that

146

excessive drinking will lead to health problems, accidents, or DUI arrests. Often these connections are causally related "if I drop a glass on a cement floor it will likely break." Or that "if I combine certain chemicals this combination will result in a specific reaction." Other connections are less causal and are more of what we call a correlation. A correlation is an association between two events, but one may not necessarily cause the other. For example, "It seems that every time I wash my car, it will rain." Washing the car likely has nothing to do with the weather.

Our lucky blue dot story is the result of what is called an illusory correlation. A correlation can be useful in helping us understand relationships between two events. An illusory correlation, however, is a perceived relationship between two events where none exists. We believe that two events are related such as rubbing the blue dot and the outcome of good luck. Not only could this relationship be illusory, but the more insidious implication is that we make the leap to causation and now believe that rubbing the blue dot causes the outcome of good luck. Correlation now becomes causation! How does an illusory correlation take on the belief of causation? The explanation has to do with what psychologists call a confirmation bias. We look for information that confirms our beliefs but fail to look for information that disconfirms our beliefs. In all good science when we test a theory or hypothesis, we gather all information, not only the evidence that confirms the theory or hypothesis, but importantly evidence that fails to confirm the theory or hypothesis. With confirmation bias we look at only the confirmatory information, in this case only the instances where rubbing the lucky blue dot resulted in good luck. What is needed in this analysis is a report of all the times that rubbing the lucky blue dot was associated with having to replace the transmission in your car costing thousands of dollars for example. It's a simple math problem, if the side where rubbing the blue dot and bad things happened is greater than the side where good things happened, then the power of the blue dot resulting in good luck would come into doubt. We can also argue that other data points needed are to ascertain when we did not rub the blue dot and good or bad things happened, and where not rubbing the blue dot resulted in no good or bad things happening (or what we call non-events).

The Power of the Testimonial

Another explanation is that we place too much emphasis on the testimonials of others. The stories of those who rubbed the lucky blue dot and achieved wonderful things are readily published and these folks are encouraged to write to the tabloid to tell of their incredible stories–not the ones who rubbed the blue dot and the transmission of their car fell out while on their way to work. We cannot overlook the psychological power of a testimonial to influence our belief in something. If others say it worked for them, then it is possible that it will work for us. Ad campaigns rely on this technique all the time. Actors in these ads will tell you to ignore what the experts say and to believe that it worked for them. Also, by using famous people in these ads greater prestige is weighed into the consumer's assessment of whether the product is good or not. Why testimonials work is that they enhance what is called a base rate fallacy. When we look at data, we want to look at how something, whether a product, or action, such as rubbing a blue dot works for most people, (i.e., the base rate). If a claim does not work for most people, then it may require us to look a bit skeptical at it. However, the interesting power of a testimonial is that it skews all assessment of whether a claim is supported or not by data. We can think of the bad restaurant review effect. Because of social media, we must now contend with the validity of on-line reviews, whether directed toward a restaurant, video game store, or sites selling products on-line. A surprising number of these reviews are by paid actors who may have not actually visited the place on which they are reviewing. Or they may be reviews posted by one's competitor. Here just one bad review significantly affects people's perception. We can probably think of our own examples, me included. For example, when I look at the reviews of a guitar I am thinking of buying, although the reviews are generally positive, I seem to be drawn to that one review that pans the instrument. I run the risk of engaging in the base rate fallacy by paying too much attention to this one bad review and neglecting what most of the reviews say.

If you want to rub the lucky blue dot—be my guest. Just remember if good things do happen, be aware of illusory correlations, the power of a testimonial, and base rate fallacies.

* * *

The Counterfactuals of Counterfactual Thinking

We can all recall an event where we took an unnecessary foolish risk or were in a tough scrape that in hindsight thought that if the result had turned out differently, what would happen. I am reminded of a commercial that aired several years ago (I no longer remember for what product) of a person standing on a high rock looking into a pond 30 feet below where the person once dived as a child. The person is seen reflecting "I think back to the risk I took and how dangerous diving into unknown waters was!" There may be a special Providence that shines down on children and fools of which all of us have been the former and some of us have also been the latter. It could be that the event resulted in an unfortunate outcome, such as we were caught TP-ing (toilet papering) someone's lawn on Halloween, or when we were swimming might have been tempted to dive from a high point into waters that we did not know its depth or what contained therein. Regardless of the outcome, we might engage in counterfactual thinking in that the event triggers in us to construct a world of what might have been. What for example, if only we did not engage in vandalism, or what if we did dive into that water, what might have happened? We can think of other events that trigger counterfactual thinking. What if we bought that stock years ago but did not and has now become a blue-chip stock? What if we only would have asked that person out on a date but did not?

Some events easily trigger counterfactual thoughts of what might have been whereas others less so. It seems we more readily have thoughts of what might have been for those things that we could have done and did not, such as not buying a certain stock that became successful, or not asking someone on a date. On the other hand, events such as getting caught toilet papering someone's lawn on Halloween night, although regretful and possibly incurred some penalty, do not involve a lot of counterfactual thinking. Why is that? Well, there is an asymmetry in how we think about events of commission versus omission. More counterfactual thoughts are generated by omissions, where we have failed to do something. One biggest regret of omission people report that generated counterfactual thinking is that they wished they had spent more time with a friend, family member, or loved one. The reason is that an almost infinite number of outcomes can be thought of "if only" we had acted. If only I had taken piano lessons as a child or hiked across Europe when I had the chance what could have happened? Perhaps I could be playing at Carnegie Hall or have written the definitive book on hiking! If only I had spent more time with someone, we could have resolved our strained relationship, or we both would have experienced the joy of having spent more time together. Whereas, commissions, such as getting caught and having to pay a price generate fewer thoughts of what might have been, because the outcome fixed the event (i.e., paid a fine) and one can now move on from the experience or may possibly have a silver lining in that you learned something valuable from the experience.

Not only is there an asymmetry in the act (omission versus commission), but also the age of the person may be a variable. Research finds that older folks tend to regret the things they failed to do than the things they did over the years. That is, they generate more "if only..." for things they wish they could have done when younger. Perhaps now it is that many things they could have done are no longer in reach or have become more difficult or impossible to do.

Research also shows that the closer we get to the world of what might have been, not only does it trigger these counterfactual thoughts but also emotion. We see the Olympic athlete who wins the silver medal less happy than the one who wins the bronze medal. The explanation here is the silver medalist was only one step away, often measured in hundredths of a second, from winning the gold whereas not only was the bronze medalist further away from the gold but also can engage in a counterfactual world of being off the medal stand by one.

We may also understand other nuances to the emotions we experience when engaging in counterfactual thinking. Perhaps, the outcome of the act plays a role. If for instance, we find that the stock which we did not buy tanked or went blue-chip may trigger thankfulness that we indeed did not buy the stock or regret that we waited.

Often, we do not act on something because of a fear of failure or that we will be embarrassed. Or most egregious is someone telling you that you cannot do it. Asking that person out on a date or taking a chance at singing in public may result in rejection. But keep in mind we now have learned something and can adjust from there. Who knows, by acting, the outcome could be positive beyond your expectations. Whereas, failing to take the chance will always leave one wondering what might have been, if only.

So, take the chance, go for it regardless of age. Of course, we do not mean the ones involving endangering life or engaging in a crime! Do not convince yourself that you cannot do something because of age, or education, or what others tell you. You can learn to play the piano, or go on hikes, or even walk all or part of the Appalachian Trail (Emma "Grandma" Gatewood did it at the age of 67!). The only regret you will experience is from not doing it.

* * *

Not Uncommon Experience

The grass is just as green.
The struggle is just as hard.
The road is just as long.
The weeds are just as deep.

The row to hoe is just as hard.
The climb is just as steep.
The pain is just as great.
The loss is just as cruel.

The sun shines through.
The moon does fall.
The clouds obscure
The shadows too.

An artist picks up light in a brush,
Flinging it to the ground.
In a shimmering splatter,
We begin again.

* * *

Chapter 8 – Closing Thoughts

In this final chapter we share our reflections on how to grow as a person, be more productive, and ultimately find joy and fulfillment in our lives. In many ways to have an uncanny grasp of the obvious places us in an intuitive and imaginative mode of consciousness, one in which we may "think like an artist." Thus, we can dance, draw, make music, paint, tell and write stories, and engage in a host of other ways to be creative. In this imaginative and unrestricted way of perceiving and thinking, we begin to feel at ease, free of worry, and experience pleasure in our creative actions. Indeed, we gain access to a form of consciousness that expands our understandings of how we may live and be. In Dean's essay, "Back to the Garden" he offers that to find peace and fulfillment is to search for those things that ground you. The flash fiction, "Epilogue: A Call from the Local Community Theater," by Dean suggests a way of resolving the conflict between getting older and one's relevance in the world. Scott offers in "Go for What You Know" to stay positive because life is the only performance you will get. In "Long Good-Byes," Dean presents a poignant look at the passing of those we love and how to let go. Finally, in "Making the Transition," Scott leads a discussion of how the decisions we make can change the trajectory of our lives, the continuity we discover when we examine our lives more closely, and how continuity and change have great implications for how we shape our future.

* * *

Back to the Garden

At times we may question what our lives are all about. We doubt our beliefs or feel we do not know what to believe in anymore, and experience a lost faith in communities, institutions, governments, even our own "standard operating procedure" for life. Lurking in the background of this existential despair, however, is an energizing life force that gives rise to many other queries: What is most important in life now? What do I believe in, and where can I find inspiration–a resurgence of hope and optimism? How do I adaptively move forward? These existential questions become instructive for revising and re-imagining how we define ourselves and how we live. They are "creative questions," requiring us to "think like an artist," asking: What might be possible? How may I continue to live meaningfully? What are the next steps in my journey? How might I return to the garden of healing and renewal–a place known for its beauty and comfort, and where hope blooms?

Such dramatic developmental challenges and adaptive transformations have occurred throughout our childhood, adolescence, and young adulthood. Furthermore, during midlife and in older age there are new periods of growth as well. As suggested by the late champion of creativity and aging, Dr. Gene D. Cohen, an outline of these transitions and metamorphoses can be found in our artistic and creative endeavors in later life. As Dr. Cohen puts forth, a first moment of transition, a Reevaluation Phase, occurs at midlife (ages 40 to 60) as we encounter a key event or experience that immerses us in a process of self-evaluation, where we reevaluate our lives, causing us to refocus, re-establish, and pursue a deeper meaning and purpose in our living. For example, a midlife reevaluation may occur when children leave home, or when relationships or jobs end, or when we are confronted by a serious illness. Later, in our sixties and seventies, changes in family responsibilities and retirement coincide with entry into a Liberation Phase, where we may feel a new psychological freedom to make life-style changes, realize a new efficacy in one's living, and further express processes of self-actualization through our creativity. In our seventies and older, our role as keepers of kith and kin are inherent in the Summing-Up Phase, where we serve as "curators of meaning" which is communicated through our approach to living, autobiographical works, story-telling, and other creative expressions. A last and final phase of growth, called the Encore Phase, is suggested to be a time of continuing to share one's insights and understanding, celebrating life and one's living, and working to leave an enduring legacy to loved ones and future generations.

As Dr. Cohen's model suggests, at every phase of our development there is possibility of a new awakening as we meet crisis, acknowledge our concerns and doubts, and hope for positive resolution. Each time, within the tumult of our uncertainty, the impetus to chart a new course, to revise and re-make ourselves, appears like a silver-lining. Indeed, the inner uneasiness we experience always offers us a new moment; a turning point where we may again re-define what we live for and begin to move beyond one's old self to become one's best self. It is a process of self-transcendence—of surrendering facets and dimensions of how we have understood and lived life, and the discovery of a rejuvenating potency that spurs us to re-create a new framework for our living. It is a process of seeking and forging new paths for personal growth and self-realization. As clinical psychologist Paul T. P Wong suggests, this re-discovery and re-orientation paradoxically may take many forms, and in older age suggests a further "ripening" where we may become more selfless, more interested and involved in giving to others, and more interested in the future and the legacy that we may leave our family, friends, and community after our death. Perhaps too, lying dormant since earlier times in our development, in later life we may become "creatively aware" and inspired again, recognizing a reservoir of untapped potential and a list of last-works-to-do. In this new awareness, in our creativity, with each brush stroke, drawn line, improvisation, story and poem, like a rose bush abloom in a late-summer garden, we realize a new beginning and vitalness in our being, and find a fresh approach to living meaningfully and imparting our legacy.

Thus, many are the moments where we will meet uncertainty about how we understand our lives and our world, and through our creative expressions seek to find renaissance in our being. Many more are the times when we may imagine a world without hate, living spontaneously and authentically as we seek to hold hope and glimpse the source of our origin. Indeed, in our artistic expressions–when we play music, reveal ourselves in dance, describe our world in a sketch or painting, or represent our hopes in stories, sewing and weaving–we may rekindle hope and become aware of the source again. It is part of us. We share it with others. It abides with us. In our creative actions we push further on into our self-discovery. As reflected in Herman Hesse's character Sinclair in his novel *Demian*, our perceptions, dreams, and interpretations of life-experiences have always mirrored back to us who we are. Our recognition of this deeper psychology leads us back to the source--to the garden–a place of comfort where we can be free to be our true self, and where we may creatively consider and imagine what is yet possible for us to be. It is a place that allows us to be who we are meant to be. But how do I start? How do I get back to the garden? It may mean listening to a new or different type of music, dancing to the beat of a new drumming, exploring a different color palette for one's paintings, or creating new patterns to sew and weave. Since childhood we have all been artists, dancers, drummers, and singers. Moreover, we have always expressed the essence of who we are in our creativity and play. And we continue to invariably tell of ourselves when we talk–it's in the glides and glissandos of our expressions as we accent and emphasize important words when we speak, in the syncopated expressions we use to convey essential meaning in our conversations, in the shaping of our phrases and the pauses that we take to breath and relax. We share our innovative life-outlook in our walk–as we shuffle across the room, or in the striding-out cadence of our exercise march, or in the careful and punctuated steps we take when we meet and greet friends. So, thinking as an artist is easy. Our existential challenges become opportunity for new songs, new dances, new sketches, new paintings, and new fiber projects, and for personal growth. Keep the pulse or play off the beat–accompany the song or the orchestra. Take the solo–move further along the path, back to the garden. In our dances and drawings, in the light and deep hues of our paintings, in the textures of our sewing and woven works, we find the place again of comfort and joy. Travel upon the path of the artist and immerse oneself in imaginative experiences and expressions. Let the creative impulse lead. It directs us back to the garden—to the source of our true self.

* * *

Epilogue: A Call from the Local Community Theater

Summertime and a world later. It is late-morning on a golden sun-drenched day, and the story's protagonist, a retired older man, is not at home. The narrative begins with the protagonist's voicemail greeting and the deuteragonist's reply.

The phone chimed and the message greeting played: "Hi, I'm not able to answer your call now, but I want you to know that as we try to resolve the most profound existential question offered by the Great Bard, 'To be—or not to be,' that friendships are the context in which the simplest of life's hopes may be nurtured and shared... I appreciate your reaching-out to me, so please leave a message and I will get back with you as soon as I can."

Softly then, a recording of "Let it Be" by the Beatles played for a few more moments before the "beep" sounded and the message ended.

"Oh, hi Mister... uhm... uhm... Oh darn! I left my tablet in the car... well anyway, this is Sheryl down at the Community Theater... and I am calling to let you know that we, the Audition Committee, would like to invite you to try out for either of the main characters' roles in Samuel Beckett's *Waiting for Godot*," the caller said.

There was a long pause. "And... I thought about our conversation from last summer, and this play really corresponds to some of the ideas you shared with me... you know... the meaning of life as we grow older... and questions about our existence and all that, you know?" She said.

Continuing, she added, "And, as I was making breakfast this morning... I glanced over and saw the memorial card for a dear family friend that hangs on our cupboard window–we have lots of photos and memorial cards that we have placed on the little windows of the cupboard..." There was a long audible exhale and pause.

"Well anyway, our friend was an engineer and loved sailing and photography. He was also a member of General Eisenhower's guard during the second World War... he had lots of stories about how the soldiers around Eisenhower operated. One reminiscence he shared with me was about when Eisenhower's guard stopped General Patton from entering an area that was restricted... General Patton didn't have the password that would allow passage and was told by the sentry to turn around and leave... he sat in his car for a moment and the sentry cocked his machine-gun... then General Patton's car left," she said.

Sheryl continued, "I loved his stories... and how with a twinkle in his eye he shared about his life and interesting experiences... always with a smile and a laugh to emphasize how folks can be hopeful... even when facing the most difficult of circumstances."

"And... I remember you saying how older people communicate and tell us something about their later life experience, even though they may never explicitly address the topic... our friend was one of those communicators for me," she added.

Sheryl went on, "I know this is getting long, but the Christmas before he died he came to a party at our house–it was a cold night and he came in and quickly moved to the fireplace to warm himself... and announced to my dad and me that he was just diagnosed with cancer–it was a shock to hear–he stood warming himself and courageously said nothing more. In the next week he would start chemotherapy and experience all the fatigue and life-disruption that goes along with having this terrible illness. I visited him once after a treatment session at his home and he talked about photography and sailing–and asked how things were going–not mentioning any of the other very serious concerns that were looming in the background... a few weeks later he died."

"He had already made all the arrangements for his funeral and interment... he didn't want to burden his family with all that," she noted.

Her voice breaking up, Sheryl continued, "He was always a happy and caring person... I remember that in passionate discussions with family and friends, he was famous for saying, 'And what can we learn from that?' I always loved how he would introduce a new perspective taking. In his photo on the cupboard he beams with a happy and warm smile... and even in those last few meetings with him... as he began chemo... he was always smiling and expressing a warmth and optimism in the moment."

She wiped a tear from her sun-blushed cheek, then closing her message Sheryl warmly said, "Well, anyway... if you are interested in the play, please call me back... and have a great day!," and then hung up.

Go For What You Know

My dream of becoming a concert pianist and to play at Carnegie Hall was dashed at 11 years of age. It came about because of my first, which was also my last, piano recital. I would say that it was my own fault for this disastrous performance because I never practiced for it. My recital piece was Tchaikovsky's "Waltz of the Flowers." It is not an easy piece, and if you never practiced, it would be downright impossible to play it well. Well, the disaster began on the first note. I failed to place my hands in the appropriate place to start the piece. So, I began playing it 4 steps above where it was supposed to start! I also recall that I played combinations of tempos outside of the ¾ waltz tempo. After about 8 or so measures, I quit playing, closed the piano lid and went back to my seat. I heard a smattering of applause, probably from my parents. My brother, also there, fared somewhat but not much better on his piece, John Philips Sousa's "Stars and Stripes." He started out strong on the introduction, that I believe everyone knows. However, after that it was a series of stops and starts, pecking and searching for the notes. He did, however, finish it much to his credit.

It is likely that many of us have been or will be in a situation that involves performing in some way. It could be giving a speech, playing a sport, or giving a musical recital. These situations involve a certain amount of stress and anxiety. Some of these preparations designed to reduce stress and anxiety are pragmatic, some are idiosyncratic, and some could be classified as superstitious. We see performers going through many rituals to get prepared for a performance. There are stories of hockey goalies who will not let anyone talk to them before a game or will step over lines on the ice rather than skate over them. Musicians not only practice scales and brief sections of the performance piece as a warmup, but most in performance situations engage in other techniques possibly to relax if feeling over-stressed, but also to get focused for the event. Many of us had the experience of a great performance, where we were "in the zone." Where everything fell into place. Frustratingly too we have had the other experience of "choking." Where everything fell apart.

When under stress or under pressure to perform we will emit our dominant response. Your dominant response will be what you typically would do in that situation. If we think of performance, athletics, art, music, etc., if you are new at it or just learning, your dominant response is to make mistakes. You are even more likely to make mistakes when you add stress to the situation. With practice you become more proficient and therefore make fewer mistakes. As you gain more expertise, your dominant response will be fewer mistakes if any and a much better performance.

If a task is easy, we are likely to perform it correctly. As a task becomes harder, our dominant response is more likely to make a mistake. This is true particularly if the task is still new to us. Or, if we never practice for it as my piano recital example attests. We might get through an easy piece of music we are sight reading with relatively few mistakes if any (perhaps playing the melody of "Mary had a Little Lamb"), but when we try to sight read a very hard piece of music, we can be sure that the odds of making more mistakes becomes greater. To turn in a good performance on a task becomes even more complicated when we add stress to the difficulty level and newness of the task at hand. Now my brother who played the introduction to "Stars and Stripes" beautifully was because he practiced and practiced this introduction so well that his dominant response became one of a great performance. However, he neglected to practice the rest of the piece with the same diligence and thus, the dominant response was to peck and plink his way through. A grim history can be written of disastrous recitals due to overwrought nerves, inadequate preparation, or both. I would also add, never put children in situations of high stress such as recitals until they are ready or have sufficiently practiced for it! Even if you ask how to get to Carnegie Hall, unless you really want to google the directions, you already know as the old joke goes: Practice, Practice, Practice!

The title of this article is "Go for What You Know." When we talk about going for what you know, we are recommending that one take an assessment not only of how they might perform a piece of music, poetry, or sport, but also how they might conduct themselves in life.

We offer three suggestions when you go for what you know. One is to play a piece of music like no one has played it that way before. Try playing the tune in a different key, a different meter, or even playing it backwards! But most important, is that when we play a piece it is indeed unique to us. It is our voice, style, technique that creates the music making it different from another's performance. We can also think about life as one that is truly our own and like no other. We can change the direction in the way our life is going. We can incorporate new positive ideas and thoughts into our views or throw out those that are unproductive and bring disharmony to our life. Thus, put all your energy, emotion, and soul not only into your playing but also into your life because it is the only performance you will get. The second suggestion is to bring your playing to a virtuoso level. I don't mean that you immediately take your playing level to that of an Itzhak Perlman on violin or an Andres Segovia on classical guitar, but that you start by playing what you already know. If it is a solo or an entire piece, play it even if it is at first, a very simple rendition. Then, over time keep working on it adding new ideas, expressions, or motifs to it. Here is where the practice, practice, practice part is important. Playing well is a process. Life too is a process. We can consider that life is something we continually practice at and understand that we need to keep working at bits and pieces of our lives with the goal of making it the best it can be. Third, even if you are just a beginner, play as soon as possible in front of and with others, even if you make mistakes. You will be able to share and understand that others too may be experiencing the same struggles, or achievements, or that they may serve as mentors and possibly life-long friends. The first band I played in we only knew one song. We set up in the driveway of my friend's house and played the song continuously for hours. Surprisingly, people stopped by to listen! Although I never made it to Carnegie Hall, this one-song concert in the driveway gave me the confidence to "go for what I know."

* * *

Long Good-Byes

As we went to see my wife's family one summer, we heard that a dear family friend was very sick. She had cancer and was not expected to survive much longer. So, it was important to pay a visit. My wife had called the day before and arranged a time when it would be okay to stop by. It would be our final meeting–a time to say thank you and good-bye–and until we meet again. As we arrived my wife said that the door would be open and that we should just go into the house. Our friend would be in her bedroom, and we would just visit for a few minutes. When we entered, we exchanged "hellos," and my wife moved and sat near her on the bed. Very affectionately, my wife asked, "How are you doing today?" The smiling reply was, "Okay... now that you are here." Then my wife began, "I wanted to come and thank you for all the things you taught me... how to make lollipops and apple-cider... and for all the care and love you shared with me." It was the beginning of a moving tribute and mutual sharing of love and concern. It was a long good-bye. And I wish it could have been even longer because I do not like losing friends. But then I feel like we are still friends–I still remember her smile, her style of thinking, her optimism and holding of hope–and feel that I still have part of her with me. It is a feeling like when we say our last "good-byes" or "I love you" to dear family members before they take their final breath. We remember those moments–the exchange of kind words and shared hopes, as well as final kisses and hugs. And it is because of those feelings and expressions, that I prefer long good-byes–I want to take and keep all the good things I have learned from each person and make their memory a part of me.

As I have moved from one birthday to the next and look back on earlier moments in life and ahead to the future, I feel a bit like the Bob Dylan song, "My Back Pages," feeling that earlier times of my life were shaped a bit by old-fashioned concerns. And now in later life, I sense a new freshness in my thinking, in how I see the world, and how each moment of the day may bring new adventure. It is a feeling that I have moved beyond earlier self-interests and the obliging conformity to various social expectations—all those metrics of development that we think are important as we go through school, start our careers, form relationships, and in how we might gauge our success in life. Where concern for climbing the career ladder or making lots of money might take precedence, and where care about what others may think about me or what I was doing was relevant to gaining their praise. I am glad to have moved somewhat beyond those expectations and ways of assessing my life. It has been a gradual process—forward, then sideways or backwards at times, then forward again—the movements of finding new equilibrium and adaptation. As we grow older it is nice to think that we can "just go with the flow." I remember an old acquaintance, who as I would share about my life pursuits in rather a selfish way would say, "And, what's in it for you?" I know that we live interdependently but thinking or holding the attitude of "always looking out for number one," or the hubris of "using others for my own ends" always confounded me—made me think that I should always be "getting" something from every social encounter or interpersonal exchange. I have taken that memory with me, to remind me that I do not want to be the kind of person that sees others as a stepping-stone to a greater form of self-indulgence or ego-gratification. Don't get me wrong—I like compliments, and I like receiving gifts and receiving my fair share. But I do not want to become friends with you just because you will give me compliments or that I can "get" something from you. I do not want to help create or live in a "getting more for me" dystopian world, or be bound up in a tit-for-tat style of living. That seems like a very shallow form of existence. And short good-byes seem very superficial too.

I have heard people say, "I do not like long good-byes!" And they probably say that because they do not want to encounter the feelings of loss or remorse that arise when we recognize that we will no longer see another person again–at least not in this life. To be sure, I would never want to be abrupt in a "last" meeting. There is a great richness in extending ourselves to others as we hold their hand and are present to them as they live out their final moments. It is a time when we start to glimpse perhaps the truest and greatest expressions of beauty, love, care, and hope. It is one of the moments in life when we feel most alive and have a sense of new opportunities for our becoming.

In the last words to a parent, grandparent, family member or friend, we may express our most authentic self by telling the person how much we love them or thanking them for all the gifts they have bestowed upon us, both in their caregiving and bringing us up, and in their sharing of their unique gifts, perspectives, values, and dreams. In those last meetings, we may also discover a deeper humility–where we see ourselves in a new light as we ask for, receive, or grant forgiveness for the times we might not have been at our best or for what we wished the other person had done for us. And in the ongoing remembrance and conversations we have with ourselves, we might feel a sense of wanting to fulfill or live up to all the great hopes and aspirations that parents, grandparents, and other teachers held for us.

In one research encounter some years ago, an older couple told me of how they had met each other in a busy and bustling area of New York City. In that first encounter, however, they both immediately knew they had to take advantage of their meeting, or else they would never see each other again. So, in that initial contact they immediately became friends and began dating and later married. Soon after they had a son and operated with all the care and hope parents have for their children. Though as children grow up and move towards being self-sufficient, parents have less and less power to direct and safeguard their children's lives. In the case of this couple, as their son left home and began living on his own, as most parents do, they worried about his well-being and ability to "make it" in life. Throughout college and afterwards, he lived a carefree lifestyle, imbibing in all the risky life-style activities available to young people. His parents provided help when he lost a job, needed money and a place to live, or needed special medical help or even a stay at a rehabilitation clinic. But by the time their son had reached his late thirties they came to acknowledge that they could not do much more to "help" him as he succumbed to alcohol addiction and its associated problems. Despite their earlier good intentions, in later life they could only hope that he would just survive and have a life that would be untroubled and that offered him some form of contentment. As we talked, I felt that their love for their son had never diminished–rather, I sensed, it had grown greater but was now veiled in an awareness of their limitations to control the future or make real their earlier hopes or dreams for their son.

As they shared what they had learned about being parents–they also passed on their understanding of what we may experience as we grow older–an awareness of our limitations, an appreciation for little things in life, and a deepening of our relationships and our love for one another. It is a remembrance that reminds me of the love, care, hopes, and dreams my parents and grandparents held for their children–and my wanting to love them back by fulfilling those hopes and dreams.

Long good-byes shared with brothers and sisters and dear friends at our last meetings also inspire us to live fully–to move forward in our self-transcendence. Just a few years ago, one older brother who struggled with chronic health ailments throughout life, in our final telephone conversation began by saying, "I am not sure I have much time left... but I want you to know that you guys are my life–my everything!" We quickly shared our expressions of love and plans to visit soon. It reminded me that we cannot put off the final moments of our living in this world, but we can share and celebrate the love we hold for those dearest to us–and in our long good-byes find richness in the deeper sense of empathy, compassion, and understanding we discover.

More recently, my wife and I received a card from a very dear friend. He started, "This past year I have neglected keeping in touch..." after which he briefly described his new life involvements and challenges. And then, as if continuing our conversation from our last meeting a few years ago, he offered us the warmth of his loving embrace as he wrote, "I want you to know I have kept you in my prayers–I do not forget you!"

So, I like long good-byes–the lasting remembrance of all the good things planned and hoped for, the happy times and challenges, and the love that was given and received. In our final words to each other, in our awareness of our last moments together, we see more clearly and experience more deeply the greatest expressions of our caregiving and love. In the very big picture, life is rather short—so let us continue to hold and comfort one another, celebrating and sharing our love and compassion as we express and, without fail, offer our long good-byes.

* * *

Making the Transition: Personal Reflections

It is funny how a casual remark made almost 40 years ago and long forgotten can come back in a moment's reflection. If a professor that one of us encountered in graduate school had not opined that we had an uncanny grasp of the obvious, would this book have been written? Why was the comment even remembered? But remembered it was, and this led us to reflect on the obvious. The astute reader may have recognized some obvious themes in this book, or they may have now only revealed themselves: practice is important, be kind, do not judge, humor is funny, we all are getting older, and ghost stories are scary, for example. But there is also a deception hidden in the obvious. The deception is that we believe what is obvious is simple, unimportant, or that all should see it the same way. Paradoxically, when something is obvious it is hidden and only becomes revealed in hindsight as we outlined in our first essay. We hope that this selection of essays has convinced the reader that when we look deeper into what on the surface appears to be obvious, we discover a more profound reality. Often there is a much more complex and dynamic story to be told.

We close this book with our own personal stories about decision-making, continuity, change, and transition. As one grows as a person, there is a continuity that exists in one's decision making and the transitions we go through in life. When we make decisions, we make them in real time. Although we may have given the decision careful consideration and weighed the alternatives, we cannot at the time be completely certain of the outcome. It is that later, in self-reflection, that we see the thread of continuity in our decisions. Thus, in hindsight we see how the decisions we made a long time ago now seem like the inevitable, maybe even obvious, contributors to our present life. But we have learned that they were not so simple or how they would determine our future. With these thoughts in mind, we tell our stories.

We consider ourselves to be two of the luckiest and most grateful people in the world. We can look back and say we have loving spouses, families, and friends, and can look toward the future with happiness and great expectations. We are active, engaged in art, and intellectually curious. We can't fully realize how events had to line up or how the decisions we made got us to where we are today as a person. It's hard to imagine that decisions made 40 or 50 years ago, or decisions made today will become the threads that are woven into the fabric that makes us who we are. Often, we do not appreciate that even seemingly small choices might have huge consequences. We're not talking about whether we choose eggs or cereal for breakfast, but those choices that seem inconsequential at the time but later may have charted the course of our future. We also contemplate important decisions, such as choosing a career, changing jobs, or buying a house, that we know will have an impact on our future. But again, we must also think about the events that lead us to those decision points, and how those decisions become part of the greater complex of events that make us who we are. We also want to think about the continuity of experience as well. Even though the uncertainty of our decision making is juxtaposed against the flux of living, we can also see an underlying continuity. We had careers as university professors. Our careers were influenced by several events, such as what graduate program to choose, whether to continue in the profession when it was hard to find a job, or what university to work at and whether to continue there or move on. However, through it all we continued to remain as academics.

Another factor that is a big part of our lives is that we are engaged musicians. Dean plays trumpet and piano and has a degree in music. I play guitar, French horn, and alto horn. I play in several community bands and a jazz duo. Here is where I personally would like to reflect on the title of this article, "Making the Transition." Way, way, WAY back I played in rock bands —everything from blues to heavy metal. I later played in country bands. I had the fortune to play with musicians from all over the United States. But over the years, I no longer felt I could play until 2 a.m. or carry the equipment. I also had the feeling I was fitting less into that scene. I always enjoyed jazz and incorporated a bit of jazzy styles even when I was playing country or rock. Jazz was my transition. I needed less equipment to carry around and it was a medium that I could gracefully "age" into. Making windmills on the guitar and jumping off amplifiers was no longer fun, physically practical, or safe. I found that playing soft chords with a bourbon on the side more to my taste. Also, I did not go to college right after high school graduation. I told my dad and mom that they would just be wasting their money as I was not ready for college. At the time, I played regularly in a band, had an additional job, and a car. What more could an 18-year-old want? At least I was honest with my parents. After about 10 years of working dead end jobs, I finally realized that I needed an education if I wanted to have a successful life. I eventually graduated from college, received my Ph.D. and began working as an academic. Through it all, I still had a love for music.

Dean relates the following: I think "transitions" begin probably at birth. Certainly, childhood events shape us and influence how we become later in life. That is true for me too. My mom recognized that each of her children were unique individuals instilling in us a sense of independence. Relationships with my siblings were important influences in my life, too. I had two older brothers, three sisters and a brother who were younger. Certainly, playing with brothers and sisters and other early socialization experiences were formative events in my development. At around age four, while waiting for dinner one evening, I felt myself to be an "existentialist," pondering the relationship between myself and the outside world. I don't think I knew what it really meant to be an existentialist at that time, but that moment of self-reflection by a four-year old is a transitional event of sorts that has continued to stay with me when I think about early childhood.

I think key in my development too were my parents and grandparents' lives–filled with hope, respect, and love–that made me feel that our whole family worked in the same medium of expression and shared a common goal–one where we all are moving closer to a moment of great beauty and ultimate transformation. For example, my mom always told me that I reminded her of her dear Uncle Bob, her dad's younger brother; he had died before I was born, so I never met him–but somehow there was a familiarity, a perception of shared characteristics, and a transcending connection.

Both my parents loved music, and I grew up in a family that shared this fondness for music. My mom and dad both believed that music and the arts expressed all those things most valuable to us: Belonging to one another; respect and unconditional regard for all people; holding hope to overcome the challenges and travails that we meet in life; and always moving nearer to a moment where we may recognize the greatest truth and beauty, and experience the sacred. My dad often brought home used musical instruments for us kids to play. Mom loved to sing songs from the 1930s and 1940s; and my grandfather, "Pop," would often request an impromptu concert of any song or musical piece that we grandchildren had recently learned. These family musical experiences and later playing in different school bands greatly influenced how I would make decisions in life.

Later in college, each time I met an influential teacher who shared both their life story and love of music, I gained new insights that became a resource for me in my life journey. One music teacher in college, Dr. Henry Orland, shared his story of immigrating to the U.S. from Europe to escape the terrible events that led up to World War II. One of his principal instructions to students was to be a "renaissance thinker," and learn about history, literature, science, and technological advancements as a way of improving one's musicianship is well remembered. The personal stories that my teachers shared, describing their own key transitional moments and powerful transforming experiences, still inform and aid me now–and still direct my current life-practices in many ways.

In college, becoming friends with other musicians was also a time of forward movement in my development. The many enjoyable Friday evening soirees discussing and playing music with friends, is a dear memory. But transitions can be complex and difficult too! During my third year in college, just before the beginning of a new Fall semester, one of my dearest musician friends became seriously ill with acute pancreatitis and suddenly died. For me–the music ceased. Losing my friend changed how I felt about music. I completed my Baccalaureate degree in Music, but lost inspiration and the motivation to become a high-school music teacher. I had other interests, and those helped distract me as I grieved and tried to look further down the road. So, with the help of family, friends, and many caring teachers, I was able to find a balance again and begin to re-map what path I might follow. Part of my decision-making at this critical moment was that I would always have music—and transitioning to a different career orientation would be an advancement beyond the feelings of loss, and a step forward in my personal growth. And, some years later, as my family is now immersed in music of all different sorts, I feel like I still have music, and in a way that is as rich and deeply satisfying as I could ever imagine.

As Dean's reflections imply our experiences are not only felt in real time but can serve as a transition point in our lives. Also, those things and people that we held dearly, such as family, friends, and career paths may no longer be there and require us to change our perspective or to make different choices. We may have to find a different way to express our passions; what to keep and what to let go. We are also evolving, and our decisions should reflect that evolution. Ultimately our goal is to live much more completely and with a renewed sense of wonder. To remain authentic is to hold on to that which keeps you authentic and to discard those things that lead to an inauthentic life. But we may need help.

As we write in an earlier essay "With a Little Help from our Friends," we may need help from time to time. Dean relates: One of the most important and transitional figures for me was a college teacher, Dr. J. Robert (Bob) Russo, whom I worked with when I was a co-instructor of his Adolescent Psychology course. A student of Carl Rogers, Dr. Russo shared his humanistic approach to psychology, emphasizing forming healthy social-emotional relationships and becoming a person as the most important goals in life.

In his research with juvenile offenders, Dr. Russo sought to enhance the self-concept of the younger person, while also hoping to modify key behaviors such as sociability for psychiatric patients who were withdrawn and regressive in their pattern of behavior. Along with a significant enhancement of self-concept of the younger persons, one of the most important findings from that research project was that those juveniles deemed "most difficult to deal with" by the school-camp staff, were rated as "the most effective helpers" by hospital staff. Further, because of their interactions with younger people, the very withdrawn psychiatric patients were rated as more socially involved.

Interestingly, at the end of my Adolescent Psychology co-teaching experience, Dr. Russo asked me "what did you learn?" I responded that "I think that maybe I could do this for a job." Truly my experience as a co-instructor with Dr. Russo was a key moment in my personal development that influenced my later decision to pursue graduate school and in becoming a professor of Psychology. So again, transition means to grow up— and to be involved in the processes of self-transcendence (e.g., moving beyond how we were or how we thought) to self-realization (e.g., being the person expressing our highest potentiality). And like my involvement with Dr. Russo, I recognize that we will meet people at different points in life that provide us with key instruction and assistance in the processes of growing up and becoming a person.

Following Dean's experience of transition, I want to report that one of my transitions occurred about 25 years ago when I joined the Shippensburg Town Band. This organization consisted of the Town band, a Swing band, and a German band. These groups play 50 or more concerts, dances, or festivals per year. I play in all three. In the German band, I play alto horn which was quite easy to pick up as I had played trumpet and French horn in high school and the notes could be played with similar fingerings. But how I joined the community band was the result of a fortuitous encounter with a fellow colleague. This colleague and I were serving on a university-wide committee at the time. In our casual discussion before a meeting, I told her I played a variety of musical instruments. She mentioned that Shippensburg had a town band and that I should join. Having found out I played French horn; she said that the band needed more horn players. I told her that although I played the horn in high school, I had not touched one in over 40 years and did not own one. Her husband had an instrument repair shop at the time and always had a variety of instruments in his shop. One day she came to the meeting carrying a French horn. She handed it to me saying, "now you have no excuse not to join." I later was able to purchase my own horn, and I have been playing in the town band for over 25 years. I later joined the German band and the Swing Band.

In these stories so far, we see where transition, continuity, and decision-making intersect. Upon further reflection, Dean offers an optimistic outlook: As I think about developing as a person, those processes where we meet and make transition, move forward, and encounter new decision-making, I see it as an additive process. That is, we don't stop being who we are—

rather new facets of who we are meant to be are unveiled as we move forward in our journey. Hopefully, we will embrace "positive" or "best" choices in the decisions we make, but optimally we will adjust as needed so that we can move closer to our true potential and live a life of integrity and be people of hope. Whatever our next steps in life may be, we will always be musicians, artists, sport fans, athletes and exercisers, but also many other things too–life is a series of many transitions–of perpetual movement through a liminal space of becoming and living anew–of novel experiences–of new adventures–of becoming our best self–and in lots of ways, we've just gotten started! Again, I am reminded of all the gifts bestowed on me by my parents, grandparents, brothers and sisters, wonderful teachers, and people like Dr. Russo. Keen to recognize the difficulty of making transitions throughout the life course, Dr. Russo's freely shared with students his personal story–one that included stealing cars in Philadelphia as an adolescent, and later, with the help of caring counselors and teachers, receiving his doctorate in Psychology and Counselor Education from Pennsylvania State University. It is a great example of how we may help each other, and despite the difficult life circumstances we may endure or less than optimal choices we may make, we can find our way again, grow as a person and find new purpose in and meaning about our lives, and become our best self. Memorably, in one of my last meetings with Dr. Russo, he told me that in his mid-50s, "he still didn't know what he wanted to be when he grew up!" As I come upon new decision points in life now, I hope to continue to embrace many of the key instructions shared by parents and teachers: We are more than the sum of all the parts and experiences that make us who we are; try to always seek out healthy social-emotional relationships; and, in our self-reflections, always seek to grow as a person. Like what Dr. Russo expressed to me about his "mid-life" reflection, I feel like I am still "in process." I want to continue to consider and explore new ideas and experiences–aware that life humbly reminds me of all the many things I still need to learn. And we are all still learning! We are free to imagine and find what each new experience may bring! So, as you sit down at the piano, pick up your guitar or begin to sing, pull out your sketch pad or paint brushes, or open your journal to write, you may think, "let's get it going and see what happens!" In these creative acts we tell of our lives, express and share our hopes, concerns and love for one another, and begin to glimpse a beauty that transforms and envelopes us in the sacred. And I think we find again that there is so much more learning and living yet to do!

My personal reflection on the topic of continuity and change and final comment is if I had not come to Shippensburg University and made a choice to go somewhere else, would I have continued in the profession? If I had not come to this university and by chance met a fellow musician at a meeting, would I be playing in a community band? If I had turned down the offer to join the town band, would I be involved in other musical activities? These are questions that cannot be answered because I now am squarely placed in the reality of the decisions I made. However, it has now become obvious to both of us that these decisions and our present status are also one of continuity–we always enjoyed playing music–and enjoyed being academics. I guess that we would most likely continue doing both in some way regardless of the choices we made and where we were. And if you have gotten this far reading this book, this piece of advice to you, the reader may now seem obvious: "Do those things that fit who you are and give you satisfaction." Although simple sounding, it is not easy for any of us. Maybe it requires hard self-reflection, difficult decisions, or a painful realization that we need to make changes in our lives. But maybe the only saving grace we have in this predicament we call life, is that we are the ones who determine our own future.

* * *

Chapter Notes

Chapter 1—The Uncanny Grasp of the Obvious

The Uncanny Grasp of the Obvious

Richard Farson, *Management of the Absurd* (Simon and Schuster, 1997), 25.

Neal J. Roese and Kathleen D. Vohs, (2012). "Hindsight Bias," *Perspectives on Psychological Science 7, no.* 5 (2012): 411- 426. https://doi.org/10.1177/1745691612454303

Arthur Conan Doyle. Sherlock Holmes in "The Boscombe Valley Mystery" (1891). Originally published in *The Strand*. Later published in a compilation titled, "T*he Original Illustrated Sherlock Holmes by Arthur Conan Doyle*. (Castle): 55.

Analog People in a Digital World: Or Why I no Longer Fear AI

I am reluctant to refer to Bob and Tally as robots because of the implied negative connotations when we translate the term robot from its Czech origins. I am grousing about loopers and drum machines tongue-in-cheek because I know people use these and other devices quite expertly and produce quite lovely music.

Cream, *Live Cream* (Atco Records, 1970. The reader is directed to listen to the first song on the album, N.S.U. Although recordings of this album can be obtained on YouTube, they are not recorded very well. We suggest that the reader obtains the vinyl or a good quality reissued CD.

A Funny Thing Happened on the Way to the Concert in the Park

Scott F. Madey and Dean D. VonDras, *Music, Wellness, and Aging: Defining, Directing, and Celebrating Life* (Cambridge University Press, 2021).

Abraham Maslow, *Toward a Psychology of Being* (Simon and Schuster, 2013)

Rollo May, *The Courage to Create* (WW Norton & Company, 1994).

Rollo May, Ernest Angle, and Henri F. Ellenberger (eds.), *Existence* (Clarion Books, 1958).

Carl R. Rogers, *On Becoming a Person* (Houghton Mifflin Company, 1961).

Natalie Rogers, Keith Tudor, Louise Embleton Tudor, and Keemar Keemar. "Person-centered Expressive Arts Therapy: A Theoretical Encounter," *Person-Centered & Experiential Psychotherapies* 11, no. 1 (2012): 31-47. https://doi.org/10.1080/14779757.2012.656407

Irvin D. Yalom, *Existential Psychotherapy* (Basic Books, 1980).

Scott F. Madey. Previously published in *Laurelin* (1974, now out of print).

Chapter 2—Music as Metaphor

Softly, Gently, Music Casts Its Spell

Theresa A. Allison, Jennie M. Gubner, Krista L. Harrison, Alexander K. Smith, Deborah E. Barnes, Kenneth E. Covinsky, Kristine Yaffe, and Julene K. Johnson, "Music Engagement as Part of Everyday Life in Dementia Caregiving Relationships at Home," *The Gerontologist 64,* no. 7 (2024): 174. https://doi.org/10.1093/geront/gnad174

Debra Bakerjian, Kristen Bettega, Ana Marin Cachu, Leslie Azzis, and Sandra Taylor, "The Impact of Music and Memory on Resident Level Outcomes in California Nursing Homes," *Journal of the American Medical Directors Association 21,* no. 8 (2020): 1045-1050. https://doi.org/10.1016/j.jamda.2020.01.103

Nai Syrian Children's Choir Premiere Hussein Jan Mohamed's Rise Children, Rise to Peace for Serenade! - *YouTube.* Accessed 17 July 2025 at https://youtu.be/NEvGl6p4v1I? si=MYRSWMpI7K8qQOqJ

Gioachino Rossini, *Guillaume Tell,* Conducted by Antonio Pappano, Performed by the Accademia Nazionale di Santa Cecilia (EMI Classics, 2011).

Jeannie Simpson, "Individualized Music Interventions for Dementia-Related Behavior Management," *Journal of Christian Nursing* 40, no. 4

(2023): 242-245. https://doi.org/10.1097/
CNJ.0000000000001093

Raquel Chapin Stephenson, *Art Therapy and Creative Aging: Reclaiming Elderhood, Health and Wellbeing* (Routledge, 2021): 123-124.

Andrew Lloyd Webber, *The Phantom of the Opera: Original Broadway Cast Recording* (Polydor Records, 1987).

Who Stole the Kishka? The Copyright Problem in Music

For a detailed analysis of the Ed Sheeran case please go to following internet sites:

Adam Neely's YouTube Videos, https://www.youtube.com/watch?v=Tpi4d3YM79Q; https://www.youtube.com/watch?v=tpzLD-SAwW8

Also see Rick Beato, https://www.youtube.com/watch?v=OOsoRtPOfRs

Siena Linton. Why 'All By Myself' sounds uncannily like Rachmaninov's Piano Concerto No. 2. Classicalfm, the Most Relaxing Music, March 12, 2024. https://www.classicfm.com/composers/rachmaninov/piano-concerto-2-all-by-myself/

J. D. Wright, "TEACHING AT PITT: Turnitin Pros, Cons, and Best Practices," *University Times 54*, no. 17 (April 29, 2022). University of Pittsburgh. https://www.utimes.pitt.edu/news/teaching-pitt-turnitin, accessed June 24, 2024.

Also give a Listen to the following:

Frankie Yankovic, *Who Stole the Kishka?* (Sony Music Entertainment Inc., 1963). Written by Walter Dana and Walter Solek. https://www.youtube.com/watch?v=XCqZQUhBBHw

Ed Sheeran and Amy Wadge, *Thinking Out Loud* (Sony Music Publishing, 2014). https://www.youtube.com/watch?v=lp-EO5I6OKA

Marvin Gaye and Ed Townsend, *Let's Get It On,* Tamala Records (Jobete Music Company, 1973). https://www.youtube.com/watch?v=tQj1kPmQXwE

Eric Carmen. *All By Myself.* Arista Records (CAM-USA, 1975). https://www.youtube.com/watch?v=iN9CjAfo5n0

Rachmaninov: Piano Concerto No. 2 (now in public domain). https://www.youtube.com/watch?v=rEGOihjqO9w

Steppenwolf: John Kay. T*ighten up Your Wig.* Dunhill Records, Inc. (Trousdale, 1968). To hear the song Tighten Up Your Wig and its reference to Junior Wells: https://www.youtube.com/watch?v=2gcNTU3n67Y

They Call Me "Guitar"

Some folks use the term "desert" island. But to me that indicates a place devoid of trees, foliage, and uninhabitable. Unless the term is in reference to an oasis, I prefer deserted island, meaning it is uninhabited but might be a nice place to be, otherwise.

Beverly "Guitar" Watkins Obituary https://www.legacy.com/news/celebrity-deaths/beverly-guitar-watkins-1939-2019-unsung-blues-guitar-legend/?_gl=1%2Aptjred%2A_gcl_au%2AODg1MDUxMzQ0LjE3MjMzMDQ4ODE. https://musicmaker.org/artist/beverly-guitar-watkins/

Sweet Home Chicago https://www.youtube.com/watch?v=OYqYCIxdo-w

Johnny "Guitar" Watson https://youtu.be/
Fkoq4Y8WymY
"Guitar" Slim https://youtu.be/fj33EGMbazY

The Fifth Dimension

Claude Alain and Kelly L. Mcdonald, "Age-
Related Differences in Neuromagnetic Brain Activity
Underlying Concurrent Sound Perception," *Journal
of Neuroscience 27*, no. 6 (2007): 1308-1314. https://
doi.org/10.1523/JNEUROSCI.5433-06.2007
Kim Armstrong, "How Sound Becomes
Music," *Association for Psychological Sciences APS
Observer 32*, no. 5 (2019): 32-36. Accessed 23 June
2025 at https://www.psychologicalscience.org/
redesign/wp-content/uploads/2019/05/
MayJune_OBS_2019-OnlineSmall.pdf.
Donald Fucci, Heather Kabler, Deborah Webster,
and Doug McColl, "Comparisons of Magnitude
Estimation Scaling of Rock Music by Children,
Young Adults, and Older People," *Perceptual and
Motor Skills 89, no. 3* (1999): 1133-1138. https://
doi.org/10.2466/pms.1999.89.3f.1133
Stefanos A. Iakovides, Vaasiliki T. H, Iliadou,
Vaasiliki T. H. Bizeli, Stergios G. Kaprinis,
Konstantinos N. Fountoulakis, and George S.
Kaprinis, "Psychophysiology and Psychoacoustics of
Music: Perception of Complex Sound in Normal
Subjects and Psychiatric Patients," *Annals of General
Hospital Psychiatry 3*, no. 1 (2004): 6. https://doi.org/
10.1186/1475-2832-3-6
Richard M. Warren and R. P. Warren, "Some Age
Differences in Auditory Perception," *Bulletin of the
New York Academy of Medicine 47*, no. 11 (1971):
1365-1377.

Felix Weninger, Florian Eyben, Bjorn W. Schuller, Marcello Mortillaro, and Klaus R. Scherer, "On the Acoustics of Emotion in Audio: What Speech, Music, and Sound Have in Common," *Frontiers in Psychology 4* (2013): 292. https://doi.org/10.3389/fpsyg.2013.00292

A Comedy of Errors

Leonard Bernstein, "Humor in Music," *Young People Concerts, Original CBS Television Network Broadcast Date: 28 February 1959* (Amberson Holdings LLC, 1959); accessed March 28, 2025 at https://www.leonardbernstein.com/lectures/television-scripts/young-peoples-concerts/humor-in-music

Victor Borge, *My Favorite Intermissions* (Doubleday, 1971).

Lily E. Hirsch, *Weird Al, Seriously* (Rowman & Littlefield Publishers, 2022).

Liam Lynch, Jack Black, and Kyle Gass, *Tenacious D in the Pick of Destiny* (Warner Brothers, 2006).

John Morreall, "Philosophy of Humor," in Edward N. Zalta & Uri Nodelman (eds.), *The Stanford Encyclopedia of Philosophy* (Fall 2024 Edition). Accessed June 24, 2025 at https://plato.stanford.edu/entries/humor/.

William Emmett Studwell, *The Americana Song Reader* (Psychology Press, 1997).

John P. Thomerson, *Parody as a Borrowing Practice in American Music, 1965-2015* (Dissertation University of Cincinnati, 2017).

Doug Van Nort, "Noise/Music and Representation Systems," *Organised Sound* 11, no. 2 (2006): 173-178.

Dean D. VonDras and Scott F. Madey, *Celebrating the Arts of Living: Pathways to Joy and Fulfillment in Later Life* (Bonheur & Rire, 2024).

Jordan R. Young, *Spike Jones on LP, CD, MP3 & DVD: A Guide to the Essentials* (Past Times Publishing Co., 2014).

I Know One Note, and I'm Going to Play it!

For an interesting and nuanced discussion on the topic of one-note playing see Adam Neely's YouTube https://youtu.be/eSuK_5zW2iM.

The examples I use of one-note playing to introduce this essay (i.e., Vinny Mazetta, Big Jay McNeely, Pete Townsend, and Neil Young) are from Adam Neely's YouTube and I give him credit here. Accessed May 21, 2024.

Madey and VonDras, *Music, Wellness, and Aging: Defining, Directing, and Celebrating Life.*

Chapter 3—Individual and Community Justice

Members Only

Dena M. Bravata, Sharon A. Watts, Autumn L. Keefer, Divya K. Madhusudhan, Katie T. Taylor, Dani M. Clark, Ross S. Nelson, Kevin O. Cokley, and Heather K. Hagg, "Prevalence, Predictors, and Treatment of Impostor Syndrome: A Systematic Review," *Journal of General Internal Medicine* 35, no. 4 (2020): 1252-1275. https://doi.org/10.1007/s11606-019-05364-1.

Of course, it is simplistic to think that all one needs to do is grunt out 10,000-25,000 hours to become an expert. Many factors are involved in reaching a high level of expertise, such as skill, training, practice, luck, culture, etc. But, regardless of how long it might take, we can agree that it requires a lot of work and time to get there.

Anders Ericsson, Robert Pool, *Peak: Secrets From the New Science of Expertise* (Houghton Mifflin, 2017).

Malcolm Gladwell, *Outliers: The Story of Success* (Little, Brown and Company, 2008).

Although They May Be Painful, They Are Not Dangerous

Interview with Stanley Milgram on Sixty Minutes (31 March 1979).

Hannah Arendt, *Eichmann in Jerusalem: A Report on the Banality of Evil, Revised and Enlarged Edition* (The Viking Press, 1964).

Dominic J. Packer, "Identifying Systematic Disobedience in Milgram's Obedience Experiments: A Meta-Analytic Review," *Perspectives on Psychological Science 5,* no. 4 (2008): 301-304. https://doi.org/10.1111/j.1745-6924.2008.00080.x

For a detailed analysis of the term enhanced interrogation, the definition of torture, and the ethical responsibilities of psychologists who participate in national security interrogations, please see, David H. Hoffman, Esq. Danielle J. Carter, Esq. Cara R. Viglucci Lopez, Esq. Heather L. Benzmiller, Esq. Ava X. Guo, Esq. S. Yasir Latifi, Esq. Daniel C. Craig, Esq., Sidley Austin LLP., "Report to the Special Committee of the Board of Directors of The American Psychological Association Independent Review Relating to APA Ethics Guidelines," National Security Interrogations, and Torture (2015).

Of course, anyone who has read Milgram's studies on obedience knows that the learner never received any electric shocks. It was all part of the ruse to make the teacher believe they were physically harming another person.

I use the terms experiment and study interchangeably. Milgram consistently used the word experiment to describe his studies. However, the term experiment is not technically correct as an experiment would have random assignment to conditions including a control condition which he did not use.

For those unfamiliar with the workings of Milgram's studies on obedience and to view the shock machine, one can consult any introductory psychology textbook for full details. Or go to https://www.simplypsychology.org/milgram.html

Seems Like 1984 Has Come Early

Joyce Hickson and Warren Housley, "Creativity in Later Life," *Educational Gerontology: An International Quarterly 23*, no. 6 (1997): 539-547. https://doi.org/10.1080/0360127970230604

Madey and VonDras, *Music, Wellness, and Aging: Defining, Directing, and Celebrating Life*.

George Orwell, *Animal Farm* (Oxford University Press, 2021).

George Orwell, *Nineteen Eighty-Four* (Penguin Classics, 2004).

Marwarid Tarin, "The Ban on Music by the Taliban and How it Affects the Lives of Young Musicians," *Global History Dialogues* (2023), accessed December 13, 2024, at https://globalhistorydialogues.org/projects/the-ban-on-music-by-the-taliban-and-how-it-affects-the-lives-of-young-musicians/

How Do We Define a Well Society?

John Dither, *The Good Doctors: The Medical Committee for Human Rights and the Struggle for Social Justice in Health Care* (Bloomsbury Publishing USA, 2009).

Amanda Holpuch, "Profit Over People, Cost Over Care: America's Broken Healthcare Exposed by Virus," *The Guardian,* 16 April, 2020.

Bruce Japsen, "United Health Group Doubles Profits as Patients Defer Care in Pandemic," *Forbes*, 16 July 2020.

National Academies of Sciences, *Engineering, and Medicine, Ending Unequal Treatment: Strategies to Achieve Equitable Health Care and Optimal Health for All* (The National Academies Press, 2024). https://doi.org/10.17226/27820.

Streaming video by Committed Sings, "Lift Every Voice and Sing." https://www.youtube.com/watch?v=ngFDy52eCZY

Chapter 4—Creativity

Putting All the Pieces Together

Hermann Bahr, "Expressionism," in Francis Frascina, Charles Harrison, and Deirdre Paul, eds.,

Modern Art and Modernism: A Critical Anthology (Sage, 1982): 165-170.

Paulo Cuelho, *The Alchemist, trans. Alan R. Clarke* (HarperOne, 1998).

Christine Mason Miller, *Desire to Inspire: Using Creative Passion to Transform the World* (North Light Books, 2011).

Jacob Needleman, *Tao Te Ching by Lao Tsu, trans. Gia Fu Feng and Jane English*, (Vintage, 1989).

Margarita Sanchez-Mazas and Laurent Licata, "Xenophobia: Social Psychological Aspects," *International Encyclopedia of the Social & Behavioral Sciences 25* (Elsevier, 2015): 802-807.

R. Keith Sawyer and Danah Henriksen, *Explaining Creativity: The Science of Human Innovation* (Oxford University Press, 2024).

Machine of Death, Upside-Down Dalmatians, and the Creative Process

A picture of the spotted Dalmatian can be found in any introductory psychology textbook, or by a search on google.

Christian McBride, "The Lowdown: Conversations with Christian," *SiriusXM Satellite Radio*; and "Jazz Night in America," *National Public Radio*.

Pat Martino, "Inside Jazz: Alphabetic Junctions," *Premier Guitar*, 19 July 2011.

Ryan North, Matthew Bennardo, & David Malki!. eds., *Machine of Death: A Collection of Stories About People Who Know How They Will Die* (Bearstache Books, 2010).

Playing Softly and "Tuning-in"

Eric Clapton, "Tears in Heaven" (Official Video), https://youtu.be/JxPj3GAYYZO?si=vTPJsEQxYnYf-hj4

Madey and VonDras, *Music, Wellness and Aging: Defining, Directing, and Celebrating Life.*

Suzanne K. Powell, "Case Management Resources: Wounded Warriors, The Music Corp, and Operation We Are Here," *Professional Case Management 22,* no. 2 (2017): 51-53. Http://doi.org/10.1097/NCM.0000000000000210

The OHMI Trust, "Case Study: Playing a Woodwind Instrument Despite Rheumatoid Arthritis - The Story of Louise Parry," *OHMI - Enabling Music-Making for Physically Disabled People.* Accessed March 24, 2025, at https://www.ohmi.org.uk/case-study-11.html

VonDras and Madey, *Celebrating the Arts of Living: Pathways to Joy and Fulfillment in Later Life.*

Coloring Outside the Lines, or Just Miles Beyond

Miles Davis and Quincy Troupe, *Miles,* (Simon and Schuster, 1990).

Play! Have Fun! Do Not Be Afraid! Suspend Judgment!

Connie Goldman (1991), "Late Bloomers: Growing Older or Still Growing?" *Generations 15* (1991): 41-44.

Janice Mason Steeves, *Bloom: On Becoming an Artist Later in Life* (Friesen Press, 2023).

VonDras and Madey, *Celebrating the Arts of Living: Pathways to Joy and Fulfillment in Later Life.*

Chapter 5—Things That Go Bump in the Night

Cats, Ghosts, and Other Creatures Bumping in the Night

Amy Bowman, S. P. C. A. Scottish, F. J. Dowell, and N. P. Evans, "The Effect of Different Genres of Music on the Stress Levels of Kennelled Dogs," *Physiology & Behavior 171* (2017): 207-215. https://doi.org/10.1016/j.physbeh.2017.01.024

Emma Bryce, "Which Animals Sing? Other than Birds?" "Life's Little Mysteries," *Live Science*, 10 October 2021. Accessed 24 June 2025 at https://www.livescience.com/do-animals-besides-birds-sing

Ian Cross, "Music and Social Being 1," *Musicology Australia 28*, no. 1 (2005): 114-126. https://doi.org/10.1080/08145857.2005.10415281

Günter Ehret and Bernd Haack, "Ultrasound Recognition in House Mice: Key-Stimulus Configuration and Recognition Mechanism," *Journal of Comparative Physiology 148* (1982): 245-251.

Richard R. Fay and Laura Ann Wilber, *Hearing in Vertebrates: A Psychophysics Databook* (Hill-Fay Associates, 1989).

Cheena Goodyear, "Snowball the Cockatoo is Blowing Scientists' Minds with His 14 Unique Dance Moves," produced by Chole Shantz-Hilkes, aired July 9, 2019, on *CBC Radio*. Accessed 24 June 2025 at https://www.cbc.ca/radio/asithappens/as-it-happens-tuesday-edition-1.5205193/snowball-the-cockatoo-is-blowing-scientists-minds-with-his-14-unique-dance-moves-1.5205199

Amanda Hampton, Alexandra Ford, Roy E. Cox III, Chin-chi Liu, and Ronald Koh, "Effects of Music on Behavior and Physiological Stress Response of Domestic Cats in a Veterinary Clinic," *Journal of*

Feline Medicine and Surgery 22, no. 2 (2020): 122-128. https://doi.org/10.1177/1098612X19828131

Aniruddh D. Patel and Steven M. Demorest, "Comparative Music Cognition: Cross-Species and Cross-Cultural Studies," in D. Deutsch, ed., *The Psychology of Music* (Elsevier Academic Press, 2013): 647-681.

D. Rendall and C. D. Kaluthota, "Song Organization and Variability in Northern House Wrens (Troglodytes aedon parkmanii) in Western Canada," *The Auk 130*, no. 4 (2013): 617-628. https://doi.org/10.1525/auk.2013.13069

Reuters, "Pianist's Velvety Tones Soothe Hungry Monkeys," *Bangkok Post*, 23 November 2020. Accessed 24 June 2025 at https://www.bangkokpost.com/thailand/general/2024207/pianists-velvety-tones-soothe-hungry-monkeys

Patrick E. Savage, Psyche Loui, Bronwyn Tarr, Adena Schachner, Luke Glowacki, Steven Mithen, and W. Tecumseh Fitch, "Music as a Coevolved System for Social Bonding," *Behavioral and Brain Sciences 44* (2021): e59. https://doi.org/10.1017/S0140525X20000333

Charles T. Snowdon, David Tele, and Megan Savage, "Cats Prefer Species-Appropriate Music," *Applied Animal Behavior Science 166* (2015): 106-111. https://doi.org/10.1016/j.applanim.2015.02.012

Jon Woodhouse, "Amid Pandemic, Marty Dread Plays on to Benefit Whale Foundation," *The Maui News*, 14 November 2020. Access 24 June 2025 at (https://www.mauinews.com/news/local-news/2020/11/amid-pandemic-marty-dread-plays-on-to-benefit-whale-foundation/

Chapter 6—Getting Older and Interpersonal

Cast as a Non-Speaking Character: A Short Story

Bert Cardullo, "Whose Town is it, Anyway? A Reconsideration of Thornton Wilder's 'Our Town'," *CLA Journal 42, no. 1* (1998): 71-86.

Macy Mcdonald, "Thorton Wilder, American Existential Playwright: Existential Themes in 'Our Town' and Sartre's 'No Exit'," in Jackson R. Bryer, Judith P. Hallet, and Edyta K. Oczkowicz, eds., *Thornton Wilder in Collaboration: Collected Essays on His Drama and Fiction* (Cambridge Scholar Publishing, 2018): 30-44.

Leo Missinne. *Reflections on Aging: A Spiritual Guide* (Liguori Publications, 1990).

Jeff Turner, "'No Curtain. No Scenery:' Thornton Wilder's 'Our Town' and the Politics of Whiteness," *Theatre Symposium 9* (Southeastern Theatre Conference and the University of Alabama Press, 2001): 107.

Thornton Wilder, *Our Town: A Play in Three Acts* (Samuel French, Inc., 1965).

How to Be Ageist

Liat Ayalon and Clemens Tesch-Romer, "Contemporary Perspectives on Ageism," *Springer Nature* (2018).

Anna Rosa Donizzetti, "Ageism in an Aging Society: The Role of Knowledge, Anxiety About Aging, and Stereotypes in Young People and Adults," *International Journal of Environmental Research and Public Health 16* (2019): 1329. http://doi.org/10.3390/ijeph16081329.

World Health Organization, "Ageing: Ageism," *Newsroom*, 28 April 2025. Accessed 25 June 2025 at https://www.who.int/news-room/questions-and-answers/item/ageing-ageism

What We Can Accomplish with a Little Help from Our Friends

Martin Buber, *I and Thou, Translated by Walter Kaufmann* (Charles Scribner's Sons, 1970).

Erik H. Erikson, Joan M. Erikson, and Helen Q. Kivnick, *Vital Involvement in Old Age* (WW Norton & Company, 1994).

Angela Glendenning, "Self, Civic Engagement and Late-Life Creativity," in David Amigoni and Gordon McMullan (eds.), *Creativity in Later Life* (Routledge, 2018): 161-164.

Susan Hogan and Emily Bradfield, "Creative Ageing: The Social Policy Challenge," in David Amigoni and Gordon McMullan (eds.), *Creativity in Later Life* (Routledge, 2018): 31-46.

Huston Smith, *The World's Religions: Our Great Wisdom Traditions* (HarperCollins, 1986).

D. D. VonDras, I. C., Siegler, L.C. Lam, S. Iwahashi, J. Wheeler, J. Parker, T.L. Haney, J.C. Barefoot, N. Clapp-Channing, R.B. Williams, Jr., & D.B. Mark, "An Observational Measure of Social Support in Older Patients," Program Abstracts: 47th Annual Scientific Meeting, "Aging Cells to Aging Populations: Dynamics of Later Life," November 18-22, 1994 (Gerontological Society of America, 1994).

Dean D. VonDras, Gregory S. Pouliot, Sylvia A. Malcore, and Shigetoshi Iwahashi, "Effects of Culture and Age on the Perceived Exchange of

Social Support Resources," The International Journal of Aging and Human Development 67, no. 1 (2008): 63-100. https://Doi.org/10.2190/AG.67.1.d

If It Is Hard, Don't Play It

Joe Pass, "If it's hard don't play it." https://www.youtube.com/shorts/1pmlWDUOcAY?feature=share.

Finding Your Sweet Spot

Christine Carter, *The Sweet Spot: How to Accomplish More by Doing Less* (Ballantine Books, 2017).

Chapter 7—The Everyday Skeptic

Fritz Heider, *The Psychology of Interpersonal Relations* (John Wiley & Sons Inc., 1958), 5.

I Only Consult Guaranteed, Authentic, Certified Psychics

Thomas Gilovich, *How We Know What Isn't So. The Fallibility of Human Reason in Everyday Life* (The Free Press, 1991).

Gustave Kuhn, Jennifer Ortega, Keir Simmons, Cyril Thomas, Christine Mohr, "Experiencing Misinformation: The Effect of Pre-exposure Warnings and Debunking on Psychic Beliefs," *Quarterly Journal of Experimental Psychology* 76, no. 6 (2023): 1445-1456. https://doi.org/10.1177/17470218221116437

Explore the controversies of extrasensory perceptions, psychics, and the supernatural in

James Randi's *An Encyclopedia of Claims, Frauds, and Hoaxes of the Occult and Supernatural,* at https://web.randi.org/encyclopedia-of-claims.html (accessed July 7, 2025).

William J. Smithey, "The Use of Psychics in Homicide and Missing Persons Investigations" (2012). https://www.fdle.state.fl.us/FCJEI/Programs/SLP/Documents/Full-Text/Smithey,-William-J-paper.aspx

Jane Ayers Sweat and Mark W. Durm, Psychics: Do Police Departments Really Use Them? *Skeptical Inquirer* 17, no. 2 (1993): 148-158.

The Blue Dot is Back! And So Are Illusory Correlations!

"The Blue Dot is Back & Sizzling With Power," *The National Enquirer*, 24 July 2023. Accessed 2 July 2025 at https://www.pressreader.com/usa/national-enquirer/20230724/282497188121353

The Counterfactuals of Counterfactual Thinking

Thomas Gilovich and Victoria Husted Medvec, "The Experience of Regret: What, When, and Why," *Psychological Review* 102, no. 2 (1995): 379-395. https://doi.org/10.1037/0033-295X.102.2.379

Victoria Husted Medvec, Scott F. Madey, and Thomas Gilovich, "When Less is More: Counterfactual Thinking and Satisfaction Among Olympic Medalists," *Journal of Personality and Social Psychology* 69, no. 4 (1995): 603-610. https://doi.org/10.1037/0022-3514.69.4.603

Chapter 8—Closing Thoughts

Back to the Garden

Gene D. Cohen, *The Creative Age: Awakening Human Potential in the Second Half of Life* (Quill, 2000).

Herman Hesse, *Demian* (In the Public Domain, 1918).

VonDras and Madey, *Celebrating the Arts of Living: Pathways to Joy and Fulfillment in Later Life.*

Paul T. P. Wong, "Self-Transcendence: A Paradoxical Way to Become Your Best," *International Journal of Existential Psychology and Psychotherapy* 6, no. 1 (2016): 9.

Epilogue: A Call from the Local Community Theater

Samuel Beckett, *Waiting for Godot: Tragicomedy in 2 Acts* (Grove Press, 1954).

John Lennon and Paul McCartney, "Let It Be," recorded by The Beatles, *On Let It Be* (Apple Records, 1970).

Long Good-Byes

Bob Dylan, "My Back Pages," from *Another Side of Bob Dylan*, Tom Wilson, producer (Columbia, 1964).

J. Robert Russo, "Mutually Therapeutic Interaction between Mental Patients and Delinquents," *Psychiatric Services 25*, no. 8 (1974): 531-533. https://doi.org/10.1176/ps.25.8.531J.

J. Robert Russo, James W. Kelz, and George R. Hudson, "Are Good Counselors Open-Minded?," *Counselor Education and Supervision 3*, no. 2 (1964): 74-77. https://doi.org/10.1002/j.1556-6978.1964.tb00359.x

Index

About the Authors

Scott F. Madey, Ph.D. is Emeritus Professor of Psychology at Shippensburg University in Pennsylvania. He plays the guitar, French horn, and Eb alto horn and is involved in the local town concert band, German band, a swing-big band and plays in a jazz duo.

Dean D. VonDras, Ph.D., is Professor of Psychology at the University of Wisconsin-Green Bay. He is a recreational musician and artist, and his research explores the psychology of aging and later life development.

www.ingramcontent.com/pod-product-compliance
Lightning Source LLC
Chambersburg PA
CBHW072128270326
41931CB00010B/1701